THE GREATEST PHYSICIAN

ON EARTH

YAHWEH RAPHA

I AM THE LORD WHO HEALS YOU

Published by Crossbridge Books
Worcester
www.crossbridgeeducational.com
© Crossbridge Books 2023
All rights reserved. No part of this publication
may be reproduced, stored in a retrieval system,
or transmitted in any form or by any means –
electronic, mechanical, photocopying, recording.
or otherwise – without prior permission of the
Copyright owner.

ISBN 978 1 913946 99 9

British Library Cataloguing in Publication Data
A catalogue record for this book is available from the British Library
Scripture taken from the New King James Version®. Copyright © 1982 by
Thomas Nelson. Used by permission. All rights reserved.

Cover design: Richard Izzard

Other Trevor Dearing titles published by Crossbridge Books:

TOTAL HEALING

GOD AND HEALING OF THE MIND

MEDITATE AND BE MADE WHOLE THROUGH JESUS CHRIST

THE GOD OF MIRACLES

IT'S TRUE

DIVINE HEALING, DELIVERANCE, AND THE KINGDOM OF GOD

WALKING WITH GOD

THE LIVING WORD – The Psalms in Everyday Life

THE LIVING WORD II – A Treasury of Devotions

THE LIVING WORD III – God's Life-Transforming Promises

THE GREATEST PHYSICIAN

ON EARTH

YAHWEH RAPHA

I AM THE LORD WHO HEALS YOU

A Biblical Study of God's Healing Power

By Rev. Trevor Dearing, MA.BD.

(1933 - 2023)

Edited by Dr R M Price-Mohr PhD

ACKNOWLEDGEMENTS

I wish to dedicate this book to the memory of Mrs Eileen Mohr, founder of Crossbridge Books and encourager of my written work. I also wish to dedicate it to Mrs Elizabeth Young who in these later years has been my main source of spiritual encouragement and practical help. I also wish to acknowledge the enormous hard work put into the production of this book by Dr Ruth Price-Mohr, especially since I have become partially sighted.

I have lots of friends who also encourage and help me, and I thank God for them, especially as I try to settle into my new environment care home from which I am still able to continue with my spiritual ministry as the Lord leads. I am also including a letter I received from Australia that typifies the way the Lord encourages me when I need it most. This will be my eighteenth book that I have written, and the letter shows how much the Lord is using them, as far away as Australia.

Yours sincerely

Trevor

"Dear Trevor,
I have read most of your books and passed them on to my friends in the church and elsewhere and had no complaints. My main observation is that you have dedicated your life to the Lord's work here on earth and I hope it will continue, health permitting and with support and prayers from people around you. The world needs especially people like you in these dark times where everything is materialistic."

CONTENTS   Page

Foreword   8
Preface   10
Introduction - In the Beginning God   12
A - The Importance of Right Belief   14
B - Believing in God   18
C - Belief in God the Creator   22
D - Believing in Heaven   27

Part 1 - Believing in the fall of man and its disastrous consequences
Chapter 1 – Sin   36
Chapter 2 - Sin enters the world   39
Chapter 3 - Sin and depravity   44
Chapter 4 - Sin and sickness   48
Chapter 5 - Sin and death   51
Chapter 6 - The endemic disease   54
Chapter 7 - Satan and suffering   59

Part 2 - God's drastic remedy for disease
Chapter 8 - The Incarnation   70
Chapter 9 - God as Saviour   81
Chapter 10 - The life and Ministry of Jesus Christ   91
Chapter 11 - The Road to Calvary   97
Chapter 12 - The Immortal Dies   101
Chapter 13 - The Resurrection of Jesus Christ   116
Chapter 14 - The Ascension of Jesus Christ   121

Part 3 - The power of the blood
Chapter 15 - The Crucifixion: the 'Power of the Blood'   130
Chapter 16 - The Blood and the Blessed Trinity   144
Chapter 17 – The Blood and the Holy Spirit   148

Part 4 - The Conclusion:
Chapter 18 – Partaking of the finished Work of God 156
Summary   169
Appendix 1 - The Nicene Creed   171

FOREWORD

It was as a young teenager that I first had the privilege of meeting Trevor. My mother, Eileen Mohr, had been attending meetings at St Paul's Church in Hainault, and on this occasion, I went with her and some of her friends. When Trevor announced the altar call, I went forward for a blessing and experienced a deep cleansing; in the words of Charles Wesley, "My chains fell off, my heart was free, I rose went forth and followed Thee."

My first experience of God's healing power that I remember was when I was about ten years old. I had terrible pain in one foot that was so bad I couldn't walk. When the doctor came, he said he had no idea what it was, and I still remember the embarrassment of having to be carried by the doctor to the bathroom because I couldn't get there by myself. The mystified doctor left and my mother, desperately wanting to help relieve me of my pain, found a prayer card that had been blessed by Brother Mandus (World Healing Crusade). She told me that he had prayed over the card so that God could heal me through his faith. At the age of ten I was easily able to accept my mother's faith in this card, joined her in prayer and waited to be healed – which of course I was. In my teen years, mainly at Trevor's meetings, I witnessed many healings. My mother herself had a healing ministry for several years.

Over the decades since, I have prayed for my pets when they have been injured, and for my children, and seen them healed. I think because pets and young children accept things that are freely offered, they can easily receive God's healing. I have never been called to a healing ministry, but on one memorable occasion I was sure that I had been called to pray for a woman to be healed. I happened to be in hospital for major surgery and whilst recovering on the ward, I became aware of another lady who had not yet been allowed home. Every morning the nurses would inspect her wound and tell her that there was infection, and she couldn't go home. The lady was clearly very distressed. After a few days, I felt a strange prompting to go and speak to her and ask her if she wanted me to pray for her. My heart was racing, but I felt very definitely that this was something I had to do even though I had no idea if she was even a Christian; I had certainly never done anything like it before – or since. So, I got out of bed, crossed the ward to her bed side and simply asked her if she wanted me to pray for her. To my astonishment she said yes! I have never been one for praying aloud, so I just said a few simple words addressed to our loving Heavenly Father to which she said, "Amen." The following morning the nurses found no sign of any infection, and, to her great relief, the lady was allowed to go home. The grateful look she cast me before she left spoke so much more than words.

Trevor's healing ministry spanned more than five decades, during which time he was the instrument of God's healing power for countless people across the generations and continents. His teaching, that has been shared in numerous books, has had a global reach, with books selling recently in India and Australia. In this, his last book, Trevor shares his lifetime's understanding and wisdom of the healing power of God in all its fulness.

Dr Ruth Price-Mohr

PREFACE

In my previous books, for example, 'Total Healing', 'Supernatural Healing Today', 'God and Healing of the Mind', 'The God of Miracles', and 'Meditate and be Made Whole', I have primarily dealt with God's healing of individuals. However, in my later years, especially through prayer, meditation, and Bible study, I have seen that this healing of individuals is only part of God's healing work, which in fact encompasses the whole life of planet earth from God's creating 'The heavens and the earth' (Genesis 1:1), to the fulfilment of His healing purpose in the creation of a new heaven and earth and His giving to human beings who believe in Him, and have committed their lives to Him, a new spiritual body, which, in His fulfilled Kingdom will never again experience pain, sickness, infirmity or even death. This present book of mine is, therefore, an attempt to describe and encompass God's healing work indicated as being part of His being and nature; His description of Himself as Yahweh Rapha (I am the Lord your Physician, I am the Lord who heals you, I am the God who heals).

I will hope to show also that even God's healing of individuals in this life is not only healing of people's illnesses or infirmities, or mental health disorders, but is aimed at making human beings, who have faith in Him, WHOLE in body, mind, and spirit, or as He also puts it in the Bible to 'Sanctify them wholly' (1Thessalonians 5:24). So, I hope to show that God's purpose and activity from the dawn of creation to the time when the establishment of a new heaven and earth is finalised. It is His real and definite purpose for humanity.

IMPORTANT NOTE

I have subtitled this book **'YAHWEH RAPHA'** in English **'I AM THE LORD YOUR HEALER'** and I use this name very often to refer to God in the book (a name revealed to Moses in the book of Exodus chapter 15:26) because I wanted to emphasise the fact that healing is deeply embodied in the name and nature of God - in His essence. So, I emphasise Yahweh's purpose and ability to heal mankind, heal individual people, and then to heal the whole of the realm of nature - bringing into being a new Heaven and a new Earth. Being a physician, or a healer, is part of the very nature of God.

> "For behold, I create new heavens and a new earth; and the former shall not be remembered or come to mind." (Isaiah 65:17)

I must remind the reader that this revelation of God as 'I AM' occurs elsewhere in the Old Testament with different suffixes denoting other aspects of God's purposes and nature in relation to Mankind. We must also note that Jesus Himself, recorded in the New Testament, often used this title in claims to be God incarnate, as you will see, especially in the part of this book about God's remedy for the endemic disease of sin affecting Mankind.

Introduction – In the beginning God

The ensuing pages of this book will only make real sense to a person who already believes in the reality of God's existence. By 'God' I mean the God and Father of our Lord Jesus Christ and God's revelation of Himself in a meaningful and final way through the ministry of Jesus, His only Son, as it is set forth in the New Testament Scriptures. I also take for granted the believers' acceptance of the whole of the Christian Bible, containing the books selected by Martin Luther at the time of the Reformation, and translated into English (in this book using the New King James version).

There are some, even sincere Christians, who regard the 'Fall of Man' as it is recorded in the Book of Genesis as mythological. I, personally, regard the books in the Bible as historical truths needing, in fact, the work of the Holy Spirit to narrate them as 'God breathed' (2 Timothy 3:16-17), since obviously, no human being was present at the time to record it, for even the account of Creation pre-dates all human history as no human being was there to record the incidents.

It is important, however, to anyone reading this book that they accept that the Fall of Man, through one man, Adam, is paramount to understanding the whole Christian Gospel message. So, Paul, in his Epistle to the Corinthians (1 Corinthians 15:21-22), states as an undeniable fact:

'Since by man came death, by Man also came the resurrection of the dead. For as in Adam all die, even so in Christ all shall be made alive.'

If I could quote a biblical text to be paramount to this present book, that indeed would be the one. Although I emphasise this text as paramount to understanding my work, I hope also, that a dubious reader will come to faith in the Lord Jesus Christ, with acceptance of Him as the Saviour of the world and their own personal Saviour, and also come to believe in the inspiration and infallibility of Holy Scripture through reading this book.

A – The Importance of Right Belief

> 'So many gods
> So many creeds
> When only a few kind words and very good deeds
> Is all this sad world needs.'

This was a poster on a billboard outside a Unitarian church in Leeds which I happened to read while I was waiting for my then fiancé Anne, to alight from a bus and come with me to my study at Wesley Theological College where I was embarking on a theological course that would lead to a London University Bachelor of Divinity Degree. I gathered that what the writer of this poster was saying to the public was that we should not put our faith in churches and their creeds to make society a better place, but rather, concentrate on helpful actions for other people. The writer seemed to be disdaining any sort of belief, and emphasising not what we believe in our heads but what we did with our hands and feet. I would, however, point out that in attempting to do this the author of the poster was in fact stating, probably without realising it, their own belief. I am sure that every human being as their thinking capacity grows, must take on, even unconsciously, some form of belief by which to live. We should note as well that the New Testament Greek word for belief 'pistuew' also means 'our faith in' or to 'trust in'.

The concept that belief is not important for human personal and corporate life is a fallacy. To take extreme examples of belief we may consider the example World

War II, 1939-1945; it's terrible destruction of thousands of lives and the bombing and levelling to the ground of many buildings and domestic homes. This war was begun partly by people in the German nations embracing the Nazi code of belief put forth by Adolph Hitler in his book 'Mein Kampf'. This man was incredibly gifted as an orator, and thousands believed they were the supreme race on earth. The incredible suffering that followed, including the massacre of Jews and other people groups, again through Nazi belief; the German invasion of Poland and other European countries; and the entry of many other nations into the war, is all recorded in history. We know that, through propaganda, belief was an important factor which propelled nations into world-wide war.

In the decades following WW2, we find the terrible suffering of many people, especially Christians in places such as China and what was the USSR, and other totalitarian states where beliefs in political dogma such as communism exist. China, as a nation, has progressed to being one of the major economies of the world; we must remember that it all began with Chinese communists believing what Mao Tse Tung said in the 'Little Red Book'.

Religious belief down the centuries has, in itself, sadly caused much division and suffering amongst human beings. We read in history for example about human sacrifice being perpetrated by religious belief that this would placate the gods. Twins and their mothers at one time were also put to death in the belief that such happenings were evil. This happened in countries with pagan religions e.g., in Africa.

In what we now call Europe, there has again been much suffering that followed the rise of Protestantism rejecting the authority and beliefs of the Roman Catholic Church. In this saga of human suffering, people were tortured to death in an attempt to make them recant their Protestant belief; people were burnt at the stake or hung drawn and quartered, in a bid to get them to renounce their Roman Catholic belief. Henry XIII famously said, "The Pope of Rome has no authority in this realm of England".

These actions, causing human suffering and death were, as I have said, often caused by extreme beliefs. I would, however, point out, that every human being is being guided and propelled in their actions by what are often unconscious beliefs. On the positive side of what belief can cause, we see many people, often those who disdain religion, giving their lives in service to the community, often in courageous and heroic ways. I myself became a Christian Minister dedicating my whole life, from the age of nineteen, to the service of God and my fellow men and women by the Christian belief I then embraced, and still embrace today. In fact, as I am writing the paragraph now, I have just finished praying for a lady in Southend who said she was very frightened by the thoughts that evil, even devilish causes were affecting her life and tormenting her mind. When she asked me to pray for her, she was obviously expressing a belief in the devil, and when I prayed for her, I was expressing my belief in the power of the Lord Jesus Christ, now risen from the dead, to overcome and banish all evil forces, from her life.

I think I have said enough to help the reader realise, if such help was needed, that belief, whether conscious or unconscious, is a dominant force in human life. I have stated in the foregoing that the words 'to believe' also means 'to have faith in' or 'to entrust to'. And if the reader examines the examples I have cited, he or she will see that it was belief becoming faith and trust, as I have been describing. So in the following pages, we shall be examining belief in God, especially in God as a Physician, and seeing what effect this belief has in corporate and individual human life.

"IN THE BEGINNING GOD".

B – Believing in God

The Bible nowhere seeks to prove the existence of God, in fact it takes His existence for granted - that is its starting point.

> 'In the beginning God created the heavens and the earth'. (Genesis 1:1)

Philosophers down the ages, however, have put forward several intellectual propositions in which they have sought to prove the existence of God, individually and collectively. Certainly, if they cannot actually do this, they do postulate very positive arguments for His existence. I will set these forth as I have understood them:

1. The cosmological argument. This states that every 'effect' must have a definite cause - the law of cause and effect. So, they argue that the existence of the universe as we know it, including planet earth, cannot have come into existence simply by itself out of nowhere and nothing; it must have had a cause. To reach the conclusion that there must have been an effect which did in fact have a cause, this they posit as an eternal being 'God'. Centuries ago, a Greek philosopher Aristotle, called this eternal being 'the unmoved mover'.

2. The teleological argument. This sets forth the notion that the cosmos as we now know it, by its very existence, demonstrates that it must have been created by design, pointing to, for example, the

existence of the human eye, showing that it has been meticulously designed and could not just have occurred simply by a random or accidental occurrence. This argument points to the fact that the creation, in every aspect, portrays the very existence of a personal, creative, designer forming everything that exists. So, in this argument, Aristotle's 'unmoved mover' becomes not just a cause or origin of creation but the existence of an incredible mind and person in its fabric. This again, philosophers believe, sets forth an argument for the existence of God.

3. The historical argument. Through anthropological study, it is argued that humans have been shown to believe in, worship, and sacrifice to, supernatural entities we can call gods or, in the end, one God, throughout their entire history. Hindus, for example, worship many deities that are believed to be behind the existence of created things like the sun and moon. Philosophers argue that it would be complete nonsense, and make human beings irrational, if they have believed this throughout the centuries, when it was in fact a false belief. Human beings therefore could be termed, as from the dawn of history till now, as being insane. So, the fact that human beings have always believed in God in some form, sets forth another argument for His existence.

4. The ontological argument. This states that human beings have always set their mind and activities on what they call 'affection'. This is seen to be the aim of every human life and the whole goal of science

and technology. The fact that we posit this perfection, philosophers say, demonstrates powerfully that there must be perfection in mind, or possibly a being who is perfect; or if there was no perfection it would make nonsense of the whole idea of perfection itself.

I have presented these four so-called 'proofs' for the existence of God, knowing that the reader may not be convinced by them, or have even heard of them, but for intellectual people, they do provide a reasonable and rational foundation for the Bible's conception of God which can only, in the end, be obtained through 'faith'.

As stated earlier, belief is very important, and it is also important to bear in mind that the word belief also means to trust or entrust. So, I myself, just one among millions, do believe in God. I must say however, my coming to this belief at the age of nineteen, was not through any intellectual discourse, and certainly I didn't even know any of the arguments I have set forth above for the existence of God, and in my experience I have to say also, that amongst the thousands of Christians I have been amongst in my life, very few have said to me that they came to believe in God through some intellectual argument or process of thought. Most of them would say, as I myself state, that I came to believe in God through some particular experience deemed to be religious, that also gave them not only a purpose, for instance the work they have undertaken, but in fact, belief in God gave meaning and purpose to the whole of their life on earth from their birth to what they would know to be, eventually, their death.

Those who believe in God not only take what I call 'a leap of faith', or I could say 'they bet their lives there is a God', then they find their belief in Him has become meaningful and the basis for their own life, and what they see to be in other lives, being lived at their time. I would state therefore, that I do not consider my belief in God to be at all irrational but rather as backed up by my reasoning, and a conviction that it has given my life purpose, which is a rational thought, for the whole of my life.

I would like to add that in the last decade or two, a course of Christian belief called 'The Alpha Course', which has been attended by many seekers after truth, at the invitation of Christian believers, sets forth in a way that can be understood, the main tenets of the Christian faith in God, including the infilling of people's lives by the Holy Spirit, and has been seen to give meaning and purpose in life to many hundreds of people who have then embraced the Christian faith and have become worshippers at Christian churches. Once again, these people, like me, would say that they have found this meaning and purpose to be entirely rational so that their new-found faith is not nonsense, but makes real sense to them, especially in their thought realm, giving credence to their Christian faith.

So, our conclusion about belief in the existence of God is that this belief and experience is only attained through the exercise of faith, and we also see that there are reasonable grounds for this belief and that it is not irrational.

C – Belief in God the Creator

Since the nineteenth century, nothing has caused so much consternation amongst Christians, and unbelief among those who reject the Christian faith, as the account of creation given by God to Moses and recorded as the account of creation in Genesis. This account, that originated, it is said, in God's description of it Himself, purports to detail actual chronological events in the creation of the world in a period of seven separate days, the seventh day being detailed to be a day of rest, or Sabbath, for human beings, because it is stated that this is a day on which God rested from all His work of creation.

In the light of what is now termed scientific knowledge, dating the origin of the earth to millions of years ago, and now accepted by most modern-day knowledgeable people, there have been several different theories about how the creation of planet earth came to pass millions and millions of years ago, and the one I knew in my grammar school days was called 'The Big Bang Theory'. I was taught that the earth's origin occurred when there was a tremendous explosion of matter emanating from a single point in the universe which then expanded and stretched to grow as large as it is right now and is still expanding. Astronomers and mathematicians have more recently developed models to speculate that at the time of the Big Bang there would have been a ten-billion-degree sea of neutrons, protons, electrons, positron, photons, and neutrinos that over time cooled and recombined. After this, over millions of years, life began on earth, eventually producing a primeval being that eventually evolved into the male and female - men and women. I have tried to keep somewhat in thought all that has been propounded today, but I must admit I have lost track of many of the details, arguments, and theories. What I would say is, that these theories, unlike the account set forth in the Bible, seem to indicate that everything that happened, which we now experience in the modern world, was 'an accident'. These theories of evolution seem to me to be much more irrational than the Biblical account by suggesting that the causes of life and its events are almost a matter of good or back luck or not in any way to have a meaningful goal. And so I find, and many others do I am sure, that these theories can cause a person to feel insecure, as though they were a mere dot on a sphere dangling somehow in space in a way which can only be described by scientists as the force of 'gravity', the origin of which they cannot likewise explain.

In thinking about the origin of the earth, some facts have pressed on my mind. One such fact is that no human being, or any imagined being, except the God we envisage, can make something out of absolutely nothing, not even having fresh air to help in creating something. Similarly, no being we can conceive other than God, can enter a vast space that is in pitch darkness, absolutely pitch darkness, and just by saying something, can make that space to be filled with brilliant light. It is rational simply to believe that God said, "Let there be light and there was light", immediately overcoming what we might call 'primeval darkness'. In evoking the rationality of such belief, I would call again on what are called 'the cosmological argument' and the 'teleological argument' for the existence of God. So, for me, belief in God the Creator as recorded in the Book of Genesis, is entirely rational and helps give meaning and purpose, and indeed direction, for the whole of my life, and the lives of many millions like me.

In considering God as Creator, it is very important briefly to examine God's creation of human beings as we know them to be today, and in so examining this, Darwin's Theory of Evolution, which has either been denied or altered by many of today's scientists, has been entirely eradicated, from one's thought. It is very sad that all the scientific theories described are often taught, for instance, to young children in schools, and to modern people, as absolute FACTS when, in fact, they are only theories which have not been absolutely proven. It is sad that because of this false teaching, many people today feel that they know about the origins of the earth and human beings as facts, denying the Biblical teaching and so negating the Bible as a book of Truth. In the Biblical account of the creation of man and wife, they are seen to be the Crown of creation, to which everything in creation is pointed towards and is to sustain.

It is therefore important to point out that in my long life I have found out that no one can account for the origin of life, and it would not be possible on any planet we have discovered so far except the Earth. The Earth itself is amazing in detail and the only planet we know that can sustain human life as we know it. This incredible detail includes for instance the earth's atmosphere with oxygen, a gas which is necessary for human life; even the speed at which the planet revolves and circumnavigates the sun has a critical distance, so important for human life that were it to be in anyway altered, human life would be impossible. At the end of His creative work, and at each stage it is quoted, 'God saw that it was good'. Why this is not always seemingly true in every detail, that it is difficult for human beings to survive in, like earthquakes and tsunamis, we shall examine in detail later in this book. In the meantime, the quotation that 'God created the heavens and the earth' makes sense of all life, including my own as I know it to be.

Other than for the fourth day, during which God made the sun, moon, and other lights in the night sky according to the Genesis account, the order of events is remarkably close to the order that today's scientists believe that the world evolved. No other religion has a creation story that is so close to modern scientific understanding or that takes an outside-of-the-universe perspective. It is clear from other passages in the Bible that when the word 'day' is used it does not necessarily mean twenty-four hours of our time, as we can see from the words of Peter:

> 'But, beloved, do not forget this one thing, that with the Lord one day is a thousand years, and a thousand years as one day,' (2 Peter 3:8)

and the words of Moses in Psalm 90:2 and 4:

> 'Before the mountains were brought forth, or ever You had formed the earth and the world, even from everlasting to everlasting, You are God.' And 'For a thousand years in Your sight are like yesterday when it is past, and like a watch in the night.'

My late wife Anne, when only an infant, attended the infant School in Barnack, a village near Stamford, which had a

Church of England foundation. This foundation meant that the local vicar was allowed to enter the school at any time by arrangement with the Headmistress for at least one lesson period to teach 'The Church of England Catechism' (the main tenets of what the Church of England believes). It was taught to the children in a question-and-answer format. One such teaching lodged itself firmly in the child's brain and belief and was sufficient for my wife to live by it, from infancy to the end of her days on earth. It was simply this:

"Who made me?"

Answer - "God made me."

"Why did God make me?"

Answer - "God made me so that I might serve Him here on earth and then enjoy Him forever in Heaven."

To this belief in Heaven, we shall now turn.

D – Belief in Heaven

I have stated in the foregoing section that believing in God the Creator has given meaning and purpose to my life, and down the centuries, to millions more. I must now state however, that for anything, or event, to be meaningful for us, we must know what 'end' goal or purpose it is serving. This word 'end' (Greek teleos, see the teleological argument), must be believed in and envisaged. We, for instance, could observe a large block of stone in front of us and a sculptor using a hammer and chisel knocking bits and pieces off it. As we look at what he is doing we will not be able to understand why a particular piece of stone is chiselled off and discarded. It would make no sense, or even nonsense, to us at the time. However, the sculptor has in mind the completed and perfected work which every knock of his hammer is going towards that particular purpose - the 'end'. Everything makes perfect sense to him because he has the end perfectly in view, and if we come back later, we will marvel at the wonderful object that earlier didn't make sense to us. We can see now what it was the sculptor had in mind to create. Similarly, it is my proposition and experience in mingling with masses of human beings, talking to many individuals, that to have a meaningful purpose in life as they live each day, they must have the 'end' to which they are living, very much in mind.

As we look at the quotation that Anne, my wife, always had in her mind, we can see that it was very important to add to the statement, 'God made me'. The extremely important reason, and what proves to be our purpose in life, was to answer the question, "WHY DID GOD MAKE

ME?" with the answer, "To enjoy Him forever in heaven". This made perfect sense to Anne as the ultimate goal for her eighty-one-year-old life. This was a conception of life of course which Anne and I shared as man and wife, and to our serving God together full time, especially in a Divine Healing Ministry, and in fact, was the basis for our life as a wedded Christian couple.

We have seen that, in our quotation from Genesis, it was stated, 'In the beginning God created the heavens and the earth'. The concept of earth, the origin of which is disputed, is very easy to understand and believe in, for it is real to us. That is, it is available to the five senses we have, either one or more of touch, taste, hearing, seeing, or smelling. For anything at all to be classified as abstract, or animal, mineral, or vegetable, it is certainly a reality in our experience and life, even though, as with radio waves, we may not be able to hear them naturally, but we know we can, given the correct apparatus to do so. However, the concept of 'Heaven' is not so available to us even as an abstract.

We describe the reality of Heaven in such words as: supernatural, spiritual, or if we want to engage in a term used by physicists, we could describe it as metaphysical. All this means is that we cannot experience it easily in a natural way, and that in the case of 'Heaven', envisaging its reality, is like a concept of God Himself or only believed in as existence by something we call faith. So, Christianity, for instance, in its total belief system, is often described as a CHRISTIAN FAITH. As we have seen in the case of my wife Anne, when such belief is taken to be a reality without reservation and unconditionally, it can and should make sense of the whole of a Christian's life; the goal towards which they envisage themselves to be headed.

The Bible itself often talks about this goal as the end and purpose of a Christian's life in such words as Paul's:

> "But one thing I do, forgetting those things which are behind and reaching forward to those things which are ahead, I press toward the goal for the prize of the upward call of God in Christ Jesus." (Philippians 3:13-14).

He also said,

> "For I am hard-pressed between the two, having a desire to depart and be with Christ, which is far better. Nevertheless, to remain in the flesh is more needful for you." (Philippians 1: 23-24), and

> "For to me, to live is Christ, and to die is gain". (Philippians 1: 21).

The author of Hebrews Chapter 12 envisaged a marathon race being run and a crowd of spectators cheering them on as they endeavour to reach the end of the race and obtain a crown as a reward, but Paul, writing to the Corinthians, also says a spiritual race ends not in an earthly crown that will fade away, but in a Heavenly crown that will never fade away, a glorious crown.

> 'Let us run with endurance the race that is set before us.' (Hebrews 12:1)

> 'Do you not know that those who run in a race all run, but one receives the prize? Run in such a way

that you may obtain it. And everyone who competes for the prize is temperate in all things. Now they do it to obtain a perishable crown, but we for an imperishable crown.' (1 Corinthians 9:24-25)

What is this Heaven like then, to which Christians aspire and that we cannot experience in any way with our earthly senses? Spiritualist mediums, in seances, often say that they can experience somebody who has died and often encourage people to believe by describing details of the dead person's dress or life. Mediums, however, cannot truthfully describe 'Heaven' in which the dead person is now living, often reporting it as a beautiful garden. Christians, however, as they believe the Bible, see this as a cruel deception. The teaching of the Bible says these so-called dead people are being contacted by someone who has, although they may not know it, 'a familiar spirit'.

The book of the Law of Moses states that all mediums must be stoned to death once discovered. There is a very detailed account of King Saul disguising himself to visit one such medium at En Dor, where he was supernaturally recognised by the medium as King Saul. The King wanted to know the outcome of a battle on the next day and the account says that the dead prophet Samuel was summoned and said to the medium,

> "Why have you disturbed me by bringing me up?" and also said to Saul that, "Tomorrow you and your sons will be with me." And the next day King Saul was killed in battle (1 Samuel 28:7-19)

In my book 'Walking with God', I have in fact set out what are occult practices, including fortune telling (see Acts 16), and I earnestly entreat all who read this book or who have the ear of fellow Christians, to urge everyone to keep away from anything that is occult, including what was called a few years ago, 'The New Age Movement'. To engage in such practices will not always result in a person being what the New Testament calls 'demonised', but these are very dangerous spiritual practices indeed that no Christian should be involved in, in any way.

Apart from this, there has been a plethora of books about 'near death experiences' where sincere people, and especially in America, have had such an experience of the 'dead'. One man I knew carried his death certificate with him. These books often describe Heaven in vivid detail as a wonderfully glorious place, not written in any way for financial gain, but often written by very knowledgeable people, like surgeons for instance, who have helped some Christians to believe in Heaven for any relative who has died in faith, and also for themselves. As I write, my own grandson has become a believer in the Lord Jesus Christ and the Christian faith, and on phoning my daughter, his mother, describing his recovery of all his Christian faith by reading such books. I would state however, that reading such a book is not the sure foundation on which Christian maturity should be based. It should be based on the Bible. I was moved by reading a quotation of the late Methodist Superintendent Minister Dr W. E. Sangster stating:

> "God has hidden the signs of heaven from us lest if we should see it in all its glory it would make life on earth unbearable."

NOTES:

1. Although I have written that in the Law of Moses it was said that mediums should be stoned to death, as with all witches, I do not think that Christians today would like or want these people to be stoned to death. It would be an act abhorrent to them. However, the fact that this was commanded in the Bible to be done, shows how serious a sin it was meant to be seen as. And so, Christians today should warn all perpetrators of these acts to renounce them and forsake them and study proper Christian acts and life as described in the Bible.

2. In Acts Chapter 16, Paul and Silas, on entering the town of Ephesus, came across a slave girl who was bringing her masters a lot of financial gain by her ability to tell fortunes. Paul did not in any way praise her for her ability, but instead cast a spirit of divination out of her and she and her masters found that she could no longer tell fortunes. The chapter further describes how when her masters saw that their hope of gain had gone, they aroused a rabble to persecute Paul and Silas.

3. The term 'metaphysical' denotes that what is physical to us and captured by our senses is not ultimately any material or solid entity at all. Matter is composed of, for example, atoms and molecules and electrical charges which, like spiritual things, are not available to our senses. Knowledge of atoms and molecules, however, does not in itself have any religious connotation, but does assist people like me

to see, that in the end, existence is not about physical things in its entirety but disappears into non-physical entities until it reaches ULTIMATE REALITY, which I, of course, call GOD.

4. It is to be noted that our Lord Jesus Christ, in teaching His people the most supreme prayer ever uttered on earth, commonly called The Lord's Prayer, addressed the prayer to, "Our Father who art in Heaven." So, we see that the name of God in this prayer is Father and the address where He dwells is in Heaven. It is also to be noted that in New Testament Greek the word for Heaven and the sky are synonymous, so Christians seem to be directed upwards as to the place where Heaven is - the description often repeated in the New Testament. It is captured simply in the children's hymn, 'There is a friend for little children above the bright blue sky'. God puts on the lips of Isaiah this same thought when He says,

> 'For thus says the High and Lofty One Who inhabits eternity, whose name is Holy; "I dwell in the high and holy place with him who has a contrite and humble spirit".' (Isaiah 57:15).

5. From the foregoing it is to be seen that, although Heaven is said to be indwelt by 'Angels and archangels', (in Isaiah Chapter 6 - cherubim and seraphim), all that Christians need to know about Heaven is that it is an eternal state of bliss, and to know that it is the place where God Himself dwells

with His Son the Lord Jesus Christ. As we have seen, Paul said of himself, "To depart and be with Christ would be far better" than this life.

PART ONE

Believing in the Fall of Man and its disastrous consequences

Chapter 1 – Sin

It is stated in the book of Genesis chapter 1, that after He had created Heaven and Earth, God saw the things which He had made, that they were very good.

> 'Then God saw everything that He had made, and indeed it was very good.' (Genesis 1:31)

This statement that 'everything was very good', cannot be borne out through human history, which begins in Genesis with Cain murdering Abel his brother and goes on to tribes and then nations eventually warring against each other, causing death and much suffering, right up to the present day in numerous parts of our contemporary world.

> 'Now Cain talked with Abel his brother; and it came to pass, when they were in the field, that Cain rose up against Abel his brother and killed him.' (Genesis 4:8)

> 'The Lord saw that the wickedness of man was great in the earth, and that every intent of the thoughts of his heart was only evil continually.' (Genesis 6:5)

We also recognise that, as far back as we can trace, there have been malevolent bacteria and viruses, and as I write this chapter it is in the midst of a global pandemic killing close to seven million people, spreading all around the world. In addition, people have had to suffer many severe illnesses, painful like cancer, and other terrible afflictions. The birth process also cannot always be described as 'very good'; certainly, it is usually painful and at times babies are born with congenital abnormalities and it is a time of high mortality for both mothers and babies, especially in poorer or more rural parts of the world.

It is also true that people suffer, time and again, from what we call 'natural disasters.' The earliest recorded is, of course, the great flood at the time of Noah in Genesis chapter 7; the next mention is a famine in the land of Canaan at the time of Abram (later known as Abraham).

> 'Now there was a famine in the land, and Abram went down to Egypt to dwell there, for the famine was severe in the land.' (Genesis 12:10)

At the time of writing there has been a terrible earthquake affecting southern Turkey and northern Syria, killing more than forty-six thousand people, and in recent months there has been extensive flooding in Pakistan and devastating wildfires as the global climate changes. It seems probable that the destruction of Sodom and Gomorrah, from which Abraham's nephew and two daughters were the only survivors, was caused by some kind of natural disaster.

Nevertheless, we can say that throughout our traceable history, the lot of human beings has very much improved, especially through the advances of medical science; and leisure pursuits have been improved by discoveries of human technology like televisions and computers. We must state however, that these have been by human endeavour, and not necessarily directly through God's inspiration. Obviously, as far back as we can trace, things have not always been, and are not today, 'very good' as described in the Book of Genesis. Something obviously has gone very wrong since God created Heaven and Earth, and the Bible, in its inspired record, seeks to show us how this has happened, and it can all be encompassed by the simple word SIN.

Chapter 2 – Sin enters the world

The word 'sin' in all its Biblical concepts is not considered to be particularly relevant to modern society, which I have seen described as 'Man Come of Age'.

Sin of course, in the Biblical concept, divides between what we would call right and wrong. However, in today's society, as far as I have seen it, the vast majority of people do not refer to the Bible as their guide, or rule book, for what is right or wrong. They regard the Bible's teaching as totally out of date. They take their reference for right and wrong almost entirely from the laws, traditions, and ideas of the society in which they live. So, for instance, whilst sex outside marriage is seen as very wrong in the Bible, especially in the books called 'Epistles', sex outside marriage is not seen as wrong in any way in modern society as long as both parties are in complete agreement to live in this way; so illicit sex in England today is very common; people describing themselves as 'partners' rather than husband and wife, although it has to be said that there are people who remain in life-long committed relationships without a certificate of marriage.

In my experience however, it is very widespread, and I cannot say that this particular idea and manner of life has proved to be happy. For instance, split-ups between partners and divorces are extremely common, often with a lot of suffering involved, especially on the part of the children, about whom, one infant teacher said to me, "Out of my class of thirty children only one child knows who their father is", and the children described the frequent procession of males through their house as 'uncles'. There are increasing cases, especially of women, being assaulted in their homes by men who they thought were in love with them. And so, the problems of such abuse of adults in their homes is all the time rapidly on the increase. Often these relationships are based mainly on sexual attraction and, in my experience, even arranged marriages, for example amongst Hindus, often prove happier than the libertarian manner in Western society.

So, with all this in mind, and much more that I could have described, we turn to the Biblical teaching for what went wrong soon after God created Heaven and Earth, and this involves the account of our first parents, Adam (the word Adam in Hebrew simply means Man) and Eve (originally 'chava' in Hebrew which means 'life'), the woman who was derived from his body to be his companion.

It is to be noted that in the Biblical account, man and woman were separate creations by God in their entirety and their being was not the result of any process, such as evolution. Consider the unique nature of humans; they alone in creation can create something new – not just tools such as some other animals do – but works of art, literature, music, engineering, mathematics and so on. It has to be noted also that their being was derived from an actual world that they belonged to and over which they had to rule, as we read in Genesis 2:7 and 1:28,

> 'And the Lord God formed man of the dust of the ground and breathed into his nostrils the breath of life; and man became a living being.'

'Then God blessed them, and God said to them, "Be fruitful and multiply; fill the earth and subdue it; have dominion over the fish of the sea, over the birds of the air, and over every living thing that moves on the earth.'

On Ash Wednesday, in many Roman Catholic orientated churches, the imposition of ashes in the shape of a cross on each forehead of worshippers is accompanied by the solemn words, "From dust you came and to dust you will return", a statement which is certainly very true.

It is taught in the book of Genesis that God set this man and his wife in a beautiful garden, and it seems that God created them because He wanted fellowship of a rational kind with beings who could communicate with Him. It is further stated that God created man 'in His own image' or 'according to Our likeness' (Genesis 1:26). This does not mean for instance that God has spiritual arms and legs, but the phrase in 'His image', or 'likeness', means that man and woman had a spirit and soul in the likeness of God's spiritual being and so they were the only beings on earth who could actually communicate with God, as they did in a very intimate way in the Garden of Eden.

A very important and greatly meaningful act is to see that this fellowship with God is not in any way coerced or imposed by God on humans. God, for instance, did not create robots which were pre-programmed to love and obey Him; for then such love and obedience would be worthless and meaningless. He did in fact, give to Adam and his wife Eve, a very important spiritual gift, that is, He gave them FREE WILL with the possibility that they might disobey Him, which in fact, they did. This act of disobedience, flagrantly rebelling against the only real dictate God had given them, through their wanting to be like God in His knowledge, is called theologically the 'Fall of Man'. As a result of this act of rebellion and rejection of God's love, Adam and Eve became lost and separated from God in the Garden of Eden. It is written that God was still seeking fellowship with them by calling out:

> 'Then the Lord God called to Adam and said to him, "Where are you?" (Genesis 3:9)

Adam had been told that if he disobeyed God, not as seen to be simply eating an apple, but in pride, wanting to be like God Himself, he had been warned that he would surely die:

> 'And the Lord God commanded the man, saying, "Of every tree of the garden you may freely eat; but of the tree of the knowledge of good and evil you shall not eat, for in the day that you eat of it you shall surely die." (Genesis 2:16-17)

It is also to be seen, and this is very important to note, that the natural world of vegetation was also affected by this Fall, by bringing up weeds etc.:

> 'Cursed is the ground for your sake; in toil you shall eat of it all the days of your life. Both thorns and thistles it shall bring forth for you, and you shall eat the herb of the field.' (Genesis 3:17-18)

Eventually, Paul in his letter to the Romans states:

> 'For we know that the whole creation groans and labours with birth pangs together until now.' (Romans 8:22)

Those who have studied philosophy, in what I have previously described as metaphysical, see that there is a real possibility of human action drastically affecting the well-being of nature (so for instance the call today is for Climate Change to save the planet from being destroyed by man's activity). Paul also says in his letter to the Romans, that sin came into the world through the disobedience of Adam.

> 'Therefore, just as through one man sin entered the world, and death through sin, and thus death spread to all men, because all sinned.' (Romans 5:12).

Chapter 3 – Sin and depravity

When we study the Biblical doctrine of sin, we find that there are several aspects of this problem which must be viewed as affecting each other. One aspect is that through Adam's fall from grace, every human being ever born since that time has been affected and is, consequently, in what is known as a 'state of sin'. There is a clear warning about the consequences of sin in Genesis when the Lord spoke to Cain before he had committed murder:

> "If you do not do well, sin lies at the door, and its desire is for you, but you should rule over it." (Genesis 4:7)

In new terminology the state of 'sin' came from the fall of Adam, and we could describe it as being part of the human DNA. It is seen as a condition which, as we have seen, is totally incurable by any human effort. It is sometimes described by theologians as 'original sin'. This state of sin can be described as a spiritual sickness affecting the whole of human life and each individual human being. It is sometimes described as 'a disease of the spirit'; the spirit which, as we have seen, is the means by which we communicate with God. So, it is seen in the Biblical account that the immediate effect of this sin was that Adam lost his ability to communicate with God; he became lost to God.

So today, in our modern world with the education of millions of people, and their growth in knowledge and intellectual prowess, sin is still a disease that cannot be eradicated and which still, by its nature, impedes human communication with God, and is still described as a disease of spirit and soul. Charles Wesley (1762), wrote the words of a hymn that speaks of the seeds of this disease of sin, and is still sung today and still shown to be meaningful to worshipers:

> O come and dwell in me,
> Spirit of power within,
> And bring the glorious liberty
> From sorrow, fear, and sin.
>
> The seed of sin's disease,
> Spirit of health, remove,
> Spirit of finished holiness,
> Spirit of perfect love.

The first stanza is based on 2 Corinthians 3:17 that makes it clear that liberty from sin requires the presence of the Spirit of the Lord:

> 'Now the Lord is the Spirit; and where the Spirit of the Lord is, there is liberty.'

The 'seed of sin' in the second stanza is a metaphor for the sinful seed of Adam that spread to all humanity after the fall. The Spirit of God removes the disease of sin and moves us towards holiness and perfection. So, admitting that human beings cannot cure this disease, worshippers call on the Holy Spirit of God to effect the cure which by no means in themselves, can they achieve.

The fact that sin is the state of the human spirit, deep down, as it were, in his being, is described by our Lord Jesus in Matthew 15:19-21:

> "For out of the heart proceed evil thoughts, murders, adulteries, fornications, thefts, false witness, blasphemies. These are the things which defile a man."

Paul also says in his letter to the Galatian church in Galatians 5:19-21:

> "Now the works of the flesh are evident, which are: adultery, fornication, uncleanness, lewdness, idolatry, sorcery, hatred, contentions, jealousies, outbursts of wrath, selfish ambitions, dissensions, heresies, envy, murders, drunkenness, revelries, and the like; of which I tell you beforehand, just as I also told you in time past, that those who practice such things will not inherit the kingdom of God."

In a similar way, for example, a cancer of the brain produces symptoms, such as headaches or loss of memory and so on, by which it is eventually recognised, so also is the disease of sin. As we have seen from the words of Jesus and Paul, sin produces all the symptoms which they sadly list and by which the disease is recognised. So, John says in his first letter (1 John 1:8),

> "If we say that we have no sin, we deceive ourselves, and the truth is not in us."

Paul, in his letter to the Romans, after examining the sorry state of the human race, both Jew and Gentile, says in Romans 3:23:

> "For all have sinned and fall short of the glory of God."

The sins they have listed of word, deed, and attitude, often manifest themselves in what we call our conscience, through which, in its pure state, we have the feeling, 'I ought to' or 'I ought not to'.

The philosopher Immanuel Kant (1724-1804) said that this feeling of 'I ought', to him, proved the existence of God because only God could have planted it in the human mind. It is to be noted however, that even the conscience can be made less or more sensitive by the way a person obeys or disobeys it's dictates. This fact is also noted by the Biblical writers and Paul quotes from Psalm 95:7-8, saying,

> 'While it is said: "Today, if you hear His voice, do not harden your hearts as in the rebellion." (Hebrews 3:15)

So once again this hardening of the conscience to dull its effects of recognising right and wrong is seen to be a fact from time immemorial. We shall, in the ensuing pages see how the Biblical writers advise us to deal with this deep problem of Sin and its ensuing sins, so that we can again have communication with God.

Chapter 4 – Sin and sickness

As we study the connection between sin and sickness, a number of factors about sin must be considered. One factor is that sin can bring sickness into the human mind (Greek 'soul' and also 'psyche', from which we get our word psychology). In Biblical times, we read in the New Testament, our Lord Jesus Christ sometimes indicated that a sickness or disability ensued from sin in the person who was so affected. So, in one case of a crippled man who was let down through the roof to the feet of Jesus by his friends, Jesus told the man his sins were forgiven:

> 'Then they came to Him, bringing a paralytic who was carried by four men. And when they could not come near Him because of the crowd, they uncovered the roof where He was. So when they had broken through, they let down the bed on which the paralytic was lying. When Jesus saw their faith, He said to the paralytic, "Son, your sins are forgiven you." (Mark 2:3-5)

When the Pharisees were critical, thinking to themselves that only God could forgive sins, Jesus told them that it didn't really matter because they could see that by forgiving this man his sins, He had cured him of his infirmity:

> "Why are you reasoning in your hearts? Which is easier to say, 'Your sins are forgiven you,' or to say, 'Rise up and walk?' But that you may know that the Son of Man has power on earth to forgive sins," He

said to the man who was paralysed, "I say to you, arise, take up your bed, and go to your house." Immediately he rose up before them, took up what he had been lying on, and departed to his own house, glorifying God.' (Luke 5:22-25)

On another occasion, when a man at the Pool of Bethesda, who could not walk, was cured by Jesus, He told him to stop sinning:

> 'Afterward, Jesus found him in the temple and said to him, "See, you have been made well. Sin no more, lest a worse thing come upon you.' (John 5:14)

This equating sickness or infirmity with sin occurred also when the disciples saw a man who had been born blind. Again, thinking about sin causing sickness, in this case the inability to see, they were very puzzled and questioned Jesus:

> 'Now as Jesus passed by, He saw a man who was blind from birth. And His disciples asked Him, saying, "Rabbi, who sinned, this man or his parents, that he was born blind?" Jesus answered, "Neither this man nor his parents sinned, but that the works of God should be revealed in him." (John 9:1-3)

Obviously, to them the man's sin could not have been the cause of his blindness because the man had been born blind, being born before he could ever have sinned. They thought it must have been the fault of his parents who had sinned. Jesus said, however, on this occasion it was neither the parents nor the man - it was not sin that caused the blindness. He said, in fact, that this was a special case, a unique case, brought into being so that God could display His power in this man.

In the Old Testament, the Psalmist, giving thanks to the Lord for His deliverance writes:

> 'Fools, because of their transgression, and because of their iniquities, were afflicted. Their soul abhorred all manner of food, and they drew near to the gates of death. Then they cried out to the Lord in their trouble, and He saved them out of their distresses. He sent His word and healed them.' (Psalm 107:17-20)

It is my opinion that Jesus did not equate sickness or suffering or infirmity with a definite sin on every occasion demonstrated by the sufferer. However, we have seen that sin can cause suffering, and forgiveness is necessary before a person can be healed, sometimes in body, sometimes in mind or soul. This will be important for us to study in the next chapter about God's healing power as the Great Physician.

Chapter 5 – Sin and death

It is very important also for us to see that it is sin which the Bible teaches is the cause of human beings, without exception, physically dying. So, to go back to our former quotation by Paul, he says that it is by Adam that sin entered the world and thereby death entered by sin:

> 'Therefore, just as through one man sin entered the world, and death through sin, and thus death spread to all men, because all sinned.' (Romans 5:12).

Paul also says in his letter to the Romans:

> "For the wages of sin is death" (Romans 6:23).

He also stated that,

> "Therefore, as through one man's offense judgement came to all men, resulting in condemnation, even so through one Man's righteous act the free gift came to all men, resulting in justification of life. For as by one man's disobedience many were made sinners, so also by one Man's obedience many will be made righteous." (Romans 5:18-19)

A magnificent chapter in his first letter to the Corinthians, Chapter 15, states in verse 26 that the last enemy of the human race to be destroyed by the resurrection of our Lord Jesus Christ from the dead, is death:

> 'The last enemy that will be destroyed is death.'

In verses 53-56, Paul goes on to say,

> 'For this corruptible must put on incorruption, and this mortal must put on immortality. So when this corruptible has put on incorruption, and this mortal has put on immortality, then shall be brought to pass the saying that is written: "Death is swallowed up in victory. O Death, where is your sting? O Hades, where is your victory?" The sting of death is sin, and the strength of sin is the law.'

Paul speaks about the returning glory of our Lord Jesus Christ, when we shall be able to say, 'O death where is thy sting and grave where is thy victory?' The sting of death is sin. So, when this comes to pass, we shall say 'O grave where is thy victory?'

So, we see that the most dreadful effect of sin is that it separates us from God and can bring about disease and infirmity as one of its symptoms, and that whenever we see one of our loved ones die, or face our own death, it is all because of the effects of sin permeating the whole of life and the world of nature.

We can summarise this teaching with the bold affirmation of scripture in a sentence inspired by God:

> 'For as in Adam all die, even so in Christ all shall be made alive.' (1 Corinthians 15:22)

So, we see that the fact of physical death and the consequent suffering of bereavement is the result of Adam's sin. It is to be noted that although the Bible talks about our length of life as three scores years and ten, the Bible nowhere teaches that on our seventieth birthday we should pack our bags, say farewell to our relatives, and die. Although the manner and time of our death, and how long we shall live, is not a categorical fact about a certain time, we should be ready for this event all our lives, as until the Lord Jesus returns it is certainly going to happen to every human being, without exception.

I hope I have shown how Biblically the terrible facts of disease and death have come into being to affect human beings. I also have hoped to show that again, through SIN, nations have made war against nations, desiring to conquer each other and so gain territory and land, and so the human story of man in relation to man continues to be one of suffering. Those who speak of what they see as 'Man Come of Age' has now invented weapons of mass destruction that could destroy the whole of mankind in a matter of hours, weapons causing suffering and death far in excess of the bows and arrows and spears used by men in wars thousands of years ago. Mankind has also developed much more sophisticated means of torture and, as we know, the last century has seen two of the most terrible wars inflicted by mankind upon each other.

This, Biblically, is seen to be all the result, and a catastrophe, caused by Adam's sin, the extent of which cannot be exaggerated.

Chapter 6 – The endemic disease

I have shown that the origin of sin and its presence in every human being is set forth by the Holy Spirit in His account of the fall from grace of Adam and his wife Eve. That this is a spiritual sickness encompassing every human being in history from birth to death is set forth also by the very intelligent and widespread journeys of the Apostle Paul as stated in his letter to the church at Rome, quoting from the psalms and the prophets, approximately two thousand years ago, in the words:

> "There is none righteousness, no, not one; there is none who understands; there is none who seeks after God. They have all turned aside; they have together become unprofitable; there is none who does good, no, not one." (Romans 3:10-12)

And he goes on to declare:

> 'For all have sinned and fall short of the glory of God.' (Romans 3:23)

This is what we could call 'endemic' sickness, as further elaborated and embellished in the fourth century AD by the man known as St. Augustine, one of the greatest theologians the church has ever had. He did indeed state that every human being is totally depraved. This condition is being spread through human transmission by everyone's birth. It is therefore a social condition because we are born into a family in a social context. This conclusion would be supported by the statement of King

David in Psalm 51, a Psalm in which this great Hebrew King confessed to God his sin in relation to the beautiful woman Bathsheba. David says:

> "For I acknowledge my transgressions, and my sin is always before me. Against You, You only, have I sinned, and done this evil in Your sight - that You may be found just when You speak, and blameless when You judge. Behold, I was brought forth in iniquity, and in sin my mother conceived me." (Psalm 51:3-5)

In Biblical terminology, every human being is seen as comprising a body, mind (soul), and spirit. These are not seen as sort of separate compartments in a human being, but as we would say, are interconnected, with each affecting the other; an organic whole. So, as we have seen already, in the ministry of Jesus, sin could make a person lame - completely unable to walk, as we have already read of the paralytic in Luke 5:17-25, and the paralytic of thirty-eight years at the Pool of Bethesda in John 5:2-8.

This could be argued as being a past and not present condition of the human race. However, as one who sat very frightened in an air raid shelter in the city of Hull, Yorkshire, in 1941 while bombs were exploding from German planes, setting fires all over the city each night killing many hundreds of innocent human beings, I have witnessed for myself the corporate sin of mankind. And as I write this, in the news on television there are continuing barbaric and unending wars taking place around the globe. There have been accounts of riots even in the most sophisticated countries around the world today, such as in the USA. Also, in wealthier countries many thousands of tonnes of waste food are being thrown away as garbage whilst many people in the world are starving to death. There is apparently a growing dichotomy between rich and poor in all the world. I would also add that whilst we would accept that social media has brought a lot of benefits, especially to young people, it has also been the vehicle through which much abuse has been perpetrated.

Very much in the news these days is the fact that human beings are destroying the world, especially by the burning of fossil fuels and the dumping of plastic waste into the sea so that Man is destroying the very planet, so that soon He will be unable to live on it, and the planet God made especially possible to have human life on it, is now altering, drastically, the changing weather patterns causing terrible loss of life and it is feared that Man will destroy the earth before the Politicians can do anything to help save it. The endemic disease of sin corrupts and destroys both individuals and communities of all sizes.

These few illustrations can support those of Paul and St Augustine, that there is something very wrong with the human race, although I am sure that very many well-meaning people are striving for the well-being of the greatest number.

I have cited these instances mainly in national life, but this inability to do only good things in an individual's life can be cited again in Paul's Epistle to the Romans, in which he concludes almost with a cry of anguish:

> 'For we know that the law is spiritual, but I am carnal, sold under sin. For what I am doing I do not understand. For what I will to do, that I do not

practice; but what I hate, that I do. If then, I do what I will not to do, I agree with the law that it is good. But now, it is no longer I who do it, but sin that dwells in me. For I know that in me (that is, in my flesh) nothing good dwells; for to will is present with me, but how to perform what is good I do not find. For the good that I will to do, I do not do; but the evil I will not to do, that I practice.
Now if I do what I will not to do, it is no longer I who do it, but sin that dwells in me. I find then a law, that evil is present with me, the one who wills to do good. For I delight in the law of God according to the inward man. But I see another law in my members, warring against the law of my mind, and bringing me into captivity to the law of sin which is in my members. O wretched man that I am! Who will deliver me from this body of death?' (Romans 7:14-24)

I am sure that well-meaning people all over the world would want the greatest well-being for the greatest number, both corporately and individually, to come to pass. But as I have shown, mankind has failed to achieve this, again both corporately and individually, in fact the very opposite has often happened. Perhaps all this emphasis on sin and evil could be seen as overstating the case when surely there has been some progress in recent years, both nationally and individually, and in there being present, at least of some spark of good.

I would cite John's Gospel Chapter 1 where it is stated of our Lord Jesus Christ's pre-existence in heaven:

> 'That was the true Light which gives light to every man coming into the world.' (John 1:9).

That this dreadful endemic condition of sin can in fact be cured, at least in part, we shall see in the ensuing Part Three of this book. It assumes that there is some light of good in humankind which can be addressed and form a connection between sin and Yahweh Rapha, the Greatest Physician on the Planet.

This drastic failure in humans, this sin, in the Bible terminology is called 'sickness', and such a drastic sickness needs a drastic solution.

Chapter 7 – Satan and suffering

There is one last consideration we must study and take into account when we are looking at suffering in the life of mankind, and that is the role of a being the Bible names as the devil, Satan, or Lucifer. The book of Common Prayer states, in its renunciation of all that is evil before a person is baptised, the words: 'I renounce the devil and all his works.'

The being 'Satan' is rarely mentioned in the Old Testament of the Christian Bible, first perhaps, being described as a serpent that tempted Eve, who in turn tempted Adam to disobey God; and with this temptation, setting before our first parents the possibility of eating of the tree of knowledge of good and evil, and so becoming like God Himself. Satan appealed to the couple's pride in not accepting their lowly state in the sight of God and wanting to become beings like God Himself - the desire for self-deification. This was the cause of Satan, or Lucifer, himself falling from Heaven:

> 'How you are fallen from heaven, O Lucifer, son of the morning! How you are cut down to the ground, you who weakened the nations! For you have said in your heart: 'I will ascend into heaven, I will exalt my throne above the stars of God; I will also sit on the mount of the congregation on the farthest sides of the north; I will ascend above the heights of the clouds, I will be like the Most High.' Yet you shall be brought down to Sheol, to the lowest depths of the Pit.' (Isaiah 14:12-15)

We can infer from this passage that if Satan himself failed to get away with his self-deification, then mere mortal men should not imitate his shameful example that would lead to certain disaster.

The devil is seen in Scripture as a created being, and in the Old Testament, in the prophecy of Ezekiel, Satan, being an archangel, and a very beautiful one, was cast out of Heaven for his pride in himself, by the Lord God Almighty 'Jehovah':

> 'Thus says the Lord God: "You were the seal of perfection, full of wisdom and perfect in beauty. You were in Eden, the garden of God; every precious stone was your covering; the sardius, topaz, diamond, beryl, onyx, and jasper, sapphire, turquoise, and emerald with gold. The workmanship of your timbrels and pipes was prepared for you on the day you were created. You were the anointed cherub who covers; I established you; you were on the holy mountain of God; you walked back and forth in the midst of fiery stones. You were perfect in your ways from the day you were created, till iniquity was found in you.' (Ezekiel 28:12-15)

In these verses, God is addressing Himself to Satan. The description of this created being does not have horns, wear a red suit or carry a pitchfork, neither is it some sort of sinister-looking creature with pointed ears and a goatee. In verse 13 it says he was in Eden, where we know from the Genesis account that he was talking to Eve and tempting her, in the guise of a serpent. In verse 14 it says that Satan was once one of the cherubs who dwelt near the throne of God, and in verse 15 it says that he was created before iniquity was found in him – created by God. Thus, we can see it is not like the Chinese yin and yang or like the Star Wars saga with two sides of the same Force, since God created the being that became Satan. God by contrast is infinite and eternal. In Isaiah 14:13, we find an explanation of what the iniquity was that was found in Satan: self-deification – wanting to be like God.

> 'For you have said in your heart: 'I will ascend into heaven, I will exalt my throne above the stars of God; I will also sit on the mount of the congregation on the farthest sides of the north; I will ascend above the heights of the clouds, I will be like the Most High.' (Isaiah 14:13-14)

We know from the account in the Acts of the Apostles that King Herod Agrippa fell into the same trap:

> 'So on a set day Herod, arrayed in royal apparel, sat on his throne and gave an oration to them. And the people kept shouting, "The voice of a god and not of a man!" Then immediately an angel of the Lord struck him, because he did not give glory to God. And he was eaten by worms and died.' (Acts 12:21-23)

In the New Testament account of our Lord's Ministry, Jesus stated:

> "I saw Satan fall like lightening from heaven. Behold, I give you the authority to trample on serpents and scorpions, and over all the power of the enemy, and nothing shall by any means hurt you." (Luke 10:18-19)

Thus, we can see that Satan was cast from Heaven to perform his evil deeds on earth, amongst mankind. As I have stated, we see Satan in the New Testament tempting Jesus to serve him and disobey his mission of death upon the cross and instead to worship Satan, who tempted Jesus ultimately, by offering him all the kingdoms of the world:

> 'Then the devil, taking Him up on a high mountain, showed Him all the kingdoms of the world in a moment of time. And the devil said to Him, "All this authority I will give You, and their glory; for this has been delivered to me, and I give it to whomever I wish. Therefore, if You will worship before me, all will be Yours." (Luke 4:5-7)

Satan could only do this of course, because, as he stated, all the kingdoms of the earth had been delivered to him, so that the human race is seen to be the main sphere of Satan's influence and deeds through human history to the present time.

We see Satan bent on evil deeds which would cause Job suffering in the book entitled 'Job'. The first two chapters of the book of Job, take us on a journey to Heaven where, again, all the archangels are seen to be in conference with the Lord God and the book states that Satan was also among them:

> 'Now there was a day when the sons of God came to present themselves before the Lord, and Satan also came among them. And the Lord said to Satan, "From where have you come?" So Satan answered the Lord and said, "From going to and fro on the

earth, and from walking back and forth on it." Then the Lord said to Satan, "Have you considered My servant Job, that there in none like him on earth, a blameless and upright man, one who fears God and shuns evil?" So Satan answered the Lord and said, "Does Job fear God for nothing? Have You not made a hedge around him, around his household, and around all that he has on every side? You have blessed the work of his hands, and his possessions have increased in the land. But now, stretch out Your hand and touch all that he has, and he will surely curse You to Your face!" And the Lord said to Satan, "Behold, all that he has is in your power; only do not lay a hand on his person." So Satan went out from the presence of the Lord. (Job 1:6-12)

It is worth noting that Satan in this passage speaks of walking back and forth on the earth, suggesting the form or appearance of something like a human. In the Garden of Eden, Satan is represented as a serpent but can nevertheless communicate directly with humans. When Jesus was tempted in the wilderness, there was evidently direct communication, with Satan speaking directly to Jesus. All this may seem very strange to modern readers but to myself, who has engaged in spiritual warfare against the devil and all his works, it is not so strange, because I have heard the devil, when I was going to cast him out in the name of Jesus, speak to me in human language, as he did in the ministry of Jesus in the New Testament.

In this account in Job, Satan says to the Lord God that His ideal human being, that is Job, was only righteous and obedient to God because God had 'put a hedge around him' and protected him from all possible misfortunes. Satan went on to say to God, 'Put him in my hands and he will curse you to your face.' Satan is then permitted by God to cause Job a lot of suffering, including the destruction of all Job's goods and the death of all his relatives. Job's suffering reaches its terrible climax when Satan strikes him in his body with terrible painful sores. So, as we see what Satan could do to Job who was completely innocent of any sin which caused this distress; it was Satan who had the power to order terrible natural forces, and evil human beings, to cause Job such suffering. Thankfully the book of Job ends with his complete vindication, and the possession of double the wealth he had before his suffering. We can be certain that Satan still has the power to inflict even righteous people with all the terrible ordeals with which he inflicted Job. People today, including Christians, wonder why many disasters are allowed to occur by God, yet we need to be aware of the powers which Satan still has, in this particular dispensation, until the Lord returns in Glory.

Satan is seen in Biblical teaching as the tempter of human beings, including Christians, to disobey God's laws and do evil things. In the New Testament, quite apart from his tempting of the Lord Jesus Christ for forty days and forty nights, he is seen as the perpetrator of evil, even to possess human beings for his purposes. So, we read, for example, that Jesus rebuked Peter about the purpose of His ministry:

'Then Peter took Him aside and began to rebuke Him, saying, "Far be it from You, Lord; this shall not happen to You!" But He turned and said to Peter, "Get behind Me, Satan! You are an offence to Me, for you are not mindful of the things of God, but the things of men." (Matthew 16:22-23)

Jesus also foretells Peter's threefold denial of knowing Him just before His crucifixion (Matthew 26:34), and warns Peter of his impending failure, saying,

"Simon, Simon! Indeed, Satan has asked for you, that he may sift you as wheat. But I have prayed for you, that your faith should not fail; and when you have returned to Me, strengthen your brethren." (Luke 22:31-32)

At the time of Judas going to betray Jesus to the Jewish authorities, it is said by John in his Gospel that Satan had entered the heart of Judas to betray Jesus when, after the Last Supper, Judas showed the mob, who had come to arrest Jesus in the Garden of Gethsemane, who Jesus was in person:

'And supper being ended, the devil having already put it into the heart of Judas Iscariot, Simon's son, to betray Him,' (John 13:2)

We can find another such reference in the Acts of the Apostles; when Peter was rebuking Ananias, one of the disciples who had chosen to deceive Peter, he said,

"Ananias, why has Satan filled your heart to lie to the Holy Spirit and keep back part of the price of the land for yourself?" (Acts 5:3)

In the whole Bible teaching, Satan is seen to be the arch-tempter, liar, and accuser of Christian men and women, until his eventual destruction, of him and all his angels, in the lake of burning fire at the time of the last judgement of the world by the Lord Jesus Christ:

> 'Then I saw an angel coming down from heaven, having the key to the bottomless pit and a great chain in his hand. He laid hold of the dragon, that serpent of old, who is the Devil and Satan, and bound him for a thousand years [...] Then Death and Hades were cast into the lake of fire. This is the second death, and anyone not found written in the Book of Life was cast into the lake of fire.' (Revelation 20:1-2 and 14-15)

So, even today, until that time, Satan is seen as the 'god of this age' who blinds men's minds so they cannot see the glory of God in the face of Jesus Christ:

> 'But even if our gospel is veiled, it is veiled to those who are perishing, whose minds the god of this age has blinded, who do not believe, lest the light of the gospel of the glory of Christ, who is the image of God, should shine on them.' (2 Corinthians 4:3-4).

> 'For we do not wrestle against flesh and blood, but against principalities, against powers, against the rulers of the darkness of this age, against spiritual hosts of wickedness in the heavenly places.' (Ephesians 6:12).

> 'Be sober, be vigilant; because your adversary the devil walks about like a roaring lion, seeking whom

he may devour. Resist him, steadfast in the faith, knowing that the same sufferings are experienced by your brotherhood in the world.' (1 Peter 5:8-9).

No wonder the book of Common Prayer (1662) says that we must state out aloud and emphatically the words:

'I renounce the devil and all his works.'

It is important to see in the whole of the Bible that the power of evil is not simply a force of evil, some kind of intangible dark energy; instead, evil is seen in this respect as a person. So evil is personified and shown to be evil; to think, scheme, decide, and make plans. This is partly brought out by C S Lewis in his book 'The Screwtape Letters', that I have read, although at that time I did not believe in Satan. This book convinced me of the personal power of Satan and all his evil scheming minions. Christians today do very well when they ask the Holy Spirit to reveal what Satan is doing to them and to their families, so that they look beyond other human beings to blame them for their plight, to what it truly is, Satan at work. We shall see in the ensuing chapters how God has provided for us, even now in the twenty-first century, the ability to defeat these powers when we have truly recognised them. It has been said that the Bible only tells us of Satan's existence to enable us to declare his defeat.

It is important to understand and believe that although Satan is a person with power of evil, he could not tempt, even a Christian, unless there was already sin in the person's life to which Satan could in fact appeal and address. Once again, we are back to the fact that Mankind's basic disease, which has catastrophically hindered man's progress both corporately and individually, is sin. Sin, therefore, is the one and only basic and endemic disease from which, as we will see, God, 'The Greatest Physician on the Planet', is active and able completely to cure.

PART TWO

God's Drastic remedy for disease

Chapter 8 – The Incarnation

We can see that it is more rational to believe in a creator God than not to, because, amongst the philosophical proofs for His existence, I have posited the fact that this belief gives meaning and purpose to every human life in particular, and the existence of the human race in general. We also saw that it is rational to believe that planet Earth, the sun, the moon, and the stars were also created by God and that although other theories have been propounded, this particular belief makes more sense than any other. Theories of how the Universe evolved are not mutually exclusive of the concept of a Creator being who put everything into motion; a Creator that exists outside time and space.

We also envisaged that planet Earth was especially designed in every respect by God for His special creation, human beings, male and female, to live whole and healthy lives in relation to Him. We also saw that envisaging human life since the 'Fall', we cannot agree with the statement in the book of Genesis that, 'everything is good' because, through what we call 'sin', the whole plan for human life as God wanted it to be has been ruined, and that this 'endemic disease' has corrupted the whole world of nature, and the whole of human life, bringing about what the New Testament describes as man's last enemy, DEATH:

> 'The last enemy that will be destroyed is death.' (1 Corinthians 15:26)

In this part of the book, I endeavour to describe what God has purposed to do, and actually accomplished, doing what human beings, despite their best endeavours, could never do, i.e., to bring healing, and in fact, re-creation, to heal the whole of this disastrous consequence of sin. This particular word 'sin' is often denoted in the Old Testament in the Hebrew word 'pashar' (which in the English language means 'rebellion'). So, in the case of Adam, the first Man, this rebellion is seen to be a complete rejection of God's Will for him. In the New Testament the word 'sin' is often denoted by the Greek word 'hamartano' (meaning in English 'to miss the mark' or 'to trespass on forbidden territory'). So we see Paul, in his letter to the Roman church, stating that all human beings have 'Missed the mark of the high calling of God in Christ Jesus.'

> 'For all have sinned [missed the mark] and fall short of the glory of God.' (Romans 3:23)

So, we can see that all sin, in the end, is disobedience to God and His perfect Will and, as we have seen, this inevitably brought about disastrous consequences for the human race. With all the foregoing in mind, we can endeavour to wind the human clock back, spanning thousands of years, and imagine how the world has looked in God's eyes in poetic language:

> God saw planet earth swinging in space,
> with nature erupting in violent and destructive ways such as plagues, pestilences, storms, hurricanes, blizzards, earthquakes, and tsunamis, doomed, dashed, and bound for total destruction, either human action (global warming)
> or destruction by massive nuclear explosion.

> God saw human beings entirely corrupted and in
> the chains of sin, utterly helpless,
> wandering about spiritually blind,
> also doomed this time, to death and hell.

Amidst this dreadful situation, the whole of the Bible, especially the New Testament, speaks of God's love forever ongoing for the world He had made, and for His special creation, made to have deep communion and fellowship with Him; His children; His human beings. A particular expression of this love can be found in John's Gospel Chapter 3:16:

> 'For God so loved the world that He gave His only begotten Son, that whoever believes in Him should not perish but have everlasting life.'

It is important to understand and wonder at the special Greek word used for God's love: 'agape'. This word is used in contrast to another word sometimes used for love, but never of God's love, that is the word 'eros' from which we get our word erotic, which means sensual emotion entirely aimed at the satisfaction of the person engaged in this kind of love and having no respect for the person so loved. It is also important to contrast the word 'agape' with the word 'philos', a word that is sometimes used for love, but again, never of God's love (from which we get our word philosophy), which means the love of wisdom, a give-and-take kind of love; or Philadelphia, which means love of brother, or brotherly love, and is perhaps closer to our word 'fond' or 'fondness' for something. The word agape, however, denotes a love that is entirely given to the beloved, with no thought at all of any gain to the person who is loving, entirely based on the person so loved, even to the point of self-sacrifice of the lover; it is a love that unites and heals; it is a love of choice, not from any attraction or obligation. This is the word used by Jesus when He said,

> "Greater love has no one than this, than to lay down one's life for his friends." (John 15:13).

This theme is taken up by Paul in his letter to the Romans where it states that God demonstrated His own love toward us, in that while we were still <u>sinners</u>, even <u>enemies</u> of God, Christ died for us:

> 'But God demonstrates His own love toward us, in that while we were still sinners, Christ died for us.' (Romans 5:8)

So, we see that God loves the world with an agape, sacrificial love. It is a further wondrous fact that the word 'world' in the Greek is not the word 'geo', meaning the stuff of the world (our word geography), for example granite, limestone, or even the sea, but in this particular verse the Greek word used is 'kosmos' (from which we get our word cosmopolitan) meaning the world of human beings. A world of human beings that Paul says is enmity against God:

> 'Because the carnal mind is enmity against God; for it is not subject to the law of God, nor indeed can be.' (Romans 8:7)

So, the astounding, and in fact infallible, message of God to the human race stated by John, is that God so 'agaped' (loved with a sacrificial love) the kosmos (the human race) that He gave His only Son. Again, in poetic language we could say:

> When God saw the world and human beings lost
> in sin and all heading for total destruction,
> He spoke in the Council Halls of Heaven,
> and all the angels and archangels bowed in awe.
> as the King of Kings and Prince of Princes shouted
> for heaven's gates to be opened. The Son of God,
> amidst the cries of praise and acclamation
> on a dark black Judean night,
> swept from eternity into time and space.
> becoming a little baby thing,
> laid in a manger in a stable,

Or as put in the wonderful words of Charles Wesley:

> "Our God contracted to a span, incomprehensibly made man." *(Let earth and heaven combine, 1745)*

This is called by theologians:

The Incarnation: God becoming Man.

This amazing fact, that God, who is Spirit in essence, whilst remaining God became a man - we could say became 'flesh', is attested by the infallible words of the Bible itself. This is apparent first of all because the Bible talks about the pre-existence of the Son of God with God the Father in the Heavenly realm. John writes in his Gospel that what he calls the 'Word', was with God and was God:

> 'In the beginning was the Word, and the Word was with God, and the Word was God. He was in the beginning with God. All things were made through

Him, and without Him nothing was made that was made' (John 1:1-3)

John goes on to say that through Him all things were created that ever have been created; the same was in the beginning with God. Very importantly for our discussion, John says that this Word (the Son of God), became flesh and dwelt among us and we beheld His glory, glory as the only begotten Son of the Father, full of grace and truth:

> 'And the Word became flesh and dwelt among us, and we beheld His glory, the glory as of the only begotten of the Father, full of grace and truth.' (John 1:14)

Later in His ministry whilst on earth, the pre-existent Son of God asked His Father to glorify Him with the glory He had with Him <u>before the world began</u>.:

> 'And now, O Father, glorify Me together with Yourself, with the glory which I had with You before the world was.' (John 17:5)

Further, Paul states in his letter to the Colossians:

> 'He has delivered us from the power of darkness and conveyed us into the kingdom of the Son of His love, in whom we have redemption through His blood, the forgiveness of sins. He is the image of the invisible God, the firstborn over all creation. For by Him all things were created that are in heaven and that are on earth, visible and invisible, whether thrones or dominions or principalities or powers. All things were created through Him and for Him. And He is before all things, and in Him all things consist.

> And He is the head of the body, the church, who is the beginning, the firstborn from the dead, that in all things He may have the pre-eminence.' (Colossians 1:13-18)

The New Testament writers, especially Matthew, under the inspiration of the Holy Spirit, state how this amazing miracle of incarnation came to be. Matthew writes that the Angel Gabriel was sent from God to a holy and pious woman called Mary who was at that time engaged to be married to an older man named Joseph. This angel, Matthew says, spoke to Mary before she had any sexual relationship with Joseph, or any man, and said that she was especially chosen by God to have the Holy Spirit from God 'overshadow her' and fertilise an egg within her womb so that she would later give birth to His Son (the Virgin Birth), and that His name should be called 'Jesus' (meaning Saviour), because he would save His people from their sins:

> "And she will bring forth a Son, and you shall call His name JESUS, for He will save His people from their sins." (Matthew 1:21)

The very familiar story is that this babe was in fact born in a stable and laid in a manger, with first shepherds, and then Magi worshipping Him. This miraculous birth is not really believed to have happened by those who are sceptical of the Christian Gospel, but I would say, who can limit anything that can happen? when the God who made Heaven and Earth is fulfilling His remarkable purpose as Yahweh Rapha, to heal the world, especially humanity, of what we have described as an endemic disease.

In the New Testament there is a record of when this miraculously born baby was taken, according to Jewish law (after eight days), to be circumcised in the Temple, when two inspired people, a woman named Anna and a man named Simeon, under the inspiration of the Holy Spirit attested to the fact that this babe was very, very, remarkable, and special for the purposes of God:

> 'So he came by the Spirit into the temple. And when the parents brought in the Child Jesus, to do for Him according to the custom of the law, he took Him up in his arms and blessed God and said; "Lord, now You are letting Your servant depart in peace, according to Your word; for my eyes have seen Your salvation which You have prepared before the face of all people, a light to bring revelation to the Gentiles, and the glory of Your people Israel." […] Now there was one, Anna, a prophetess, the daughter of Phanuel, of the tribe of Asher. She was of a great age and had lived with a husband seven years from her virginity; and this woman was a widow of about eighty-four years, who did not depart from the temple, but served God with fastings and prayers night and day. And coming in that instant she gave thanks to the Lord and spoke of Him to all those who looked for redemption in Jerusalem.' (Luke 2:27-32 and 36-38)

After this time the New Testament has a sort of silence about the life of this child except for the description of His parents losing Him in a crowd on the way from the Temple when he was aged twelve years. When He began His public ministry, probably aged thirty-three, he was called Jesus of Nazareth, or Jesus the Son of Joseph. He was only called Jesus Christ (Christ meaning the 'Anointed one' or 'Messiah') when the disciple Peter, having been asked by Jesus "Who do you say that I am?", replied:

> 'Simon Peter answered and said, "You are the Christ, the Son of the Living God." (Matthew 16:16).

The fact of The Incarnation was not believed by infiltrators into the early church, called Gnostics, Douketis, or Arians. The Gnostics and Douketis had a fundamental belief that 'spirit' was so pure in itself that it could not embrace 'flesh' which they regarded as evil in itself. So they said, in one way or another, that Jesus only <u>seemed</u> to be a man. It was against these so-called heretics that John in his First Epistle wrote,

> 'That which was from the beginning, which we have heard, which we have seen with our eyes, which we have looked upon, and our hands have handled, concerning the Word of Life - the life was manifested, and we have seen, and bear witness, and declare to you that eternal life which was with the Father and was manifested to us - that which we have seen and heard we declare to you." (1 John1:1-3)

In other words, John said that Jesus was definitely a man because the disciples had experienced Him as a normal human being. The Arians could not believe that Jesus was God because they claimed that there was once a time when He was not. Such controversies as these about the person of the Lord Jesus Christ raged on in the early church for a long time until what was known as Orthodox Christianity became formulated at the Council of Nicaea on the 19th of June 325 AD, in what is called now the Nicene Creed:

> We believe in one Lord, Jesus Christ,
> the only Son of God,
> eternally begotten of the Father,
> God from God, Light from Light,
> true God from true God,
> Begotten, not made,
> of one being with the Father
> Through Him all things were made.
>
> For us and for our salvation
> He came down from heaven:
> by the power of the Holy Spirit
> He became incarnate from the Virgin Mary,
> and was made man.

The whole of this Creed, that was likely based on an earlier Syro-Palestinian source, (which I append in full at the end of this book) is said in worship by Christians worldwide, at their Mass or Holy Communion. Although most Protestant denominations of Christians do not actually say this Creed in their worship, it is apparent in documents stating their belief that they do believe what this Creed emphatically states i.e., that Jesus Christ was true Man and true God and pre-existed with God before He created the Earth. They also believe that Jesus was born of the Virgin Mary in a miraculous way. This confirms the beliefs of Orthodox Christians of all denominations and shows that the people known as Jehovah Witnesses, Christian Scientists, and

Mormons, are not regarded as Christians because they do not subscribe to the Nicene Creed statements about the person of Jesus.

I have stated that this Incarnation of the Son of God was absolutely necessary, as far as we can possibly understand, for God - Yahweh Rapha, to heal the Earth and Mankind. So, the writer to the Hebrews states emphatically that,

> '"Inasmuch then as the children have partaken of flesh and blood, He Himself likewise shared in the same, that through death He might destroy him who had the power of death, that is, the devil, and release those who through fear of death were all their lifetime subject to bondage.' (Hebrews 2:14-15).

So, having, as it were, seen the necessity of the Incarnation for Yahweh Rapha to heal mankind and the natural world, we can now move on to see the beginning of His healing work on Earth in the person and ministry of our Lord Jesus Christ.

Chapter 9 – God as Saviour

We have seen that the miraculous birth of the Person called Jesus, and very soon Jesus Christ, has been recorded, through the inspiration of the Holy Spirit, in the Gospels according to Matthew and Luke. The four most important documents in the world, and in all the history of mankind, are in the New Testament of our Bible and called: The Gospel of Matthew, The Gospel of Mark, The Gospel of Luke, and the Gospel of John. These books tell us all we need to know about the person and ministry of Jesus Christ, God our Saviour. Although I say that these books include everything we need to know for our salvation, John actually says at the end of his Gospel:

> 'And truly Jesus did many other signs in the presence of His disciples, which are not written in this book; but these are written that you may believe that Jesus is the Christ, the Son of God, and that believing you may have life in His name.' (John 20:30-31)

John also adds:

> 'This is the disciple who testifies of these things and wrote these things; and we know that his testimony is true. And there are also many other things that Jesus did, which if they were written one by one, I suppose that even the world itself could not contain the books that would be written.' (John 21:24-25)

The four Gospels certainly indicate without question that the person of Jesus Christ was definitely a man. We have seen that John says,

> 'And the Word became flesh and dwelt among us, and we beheld His glory.' (John 1:14)

Matthew and Luke also underline the fact that Jesus was a man by stating at length the genealogy of Jesus born of David's line, beginning with Abraham. This fact was important to the readers, especially Jews, who believed firmly that the Messiah would be a descendant of Abraham who was a friend of God,

> 'But you, Israel, are My servant, Jacob whom I have chosen, the descendants of Abraham My friend.' (Isaiah 41:8)

and a Son of David because David was indeed their idea of a king:

> 'The Lord has sought for Himself a man after His own heart.' (1 Samuel 13:14).

Matthew traces Jesus' line back to David (Matthew 1:1-17), and Luke goes further in tracing Jesus' line back to Adam (Luke 3:23-37). So, at the very beginning of their accounts of the life and ministry of Jesus Christ they affirm His manhood. We also see in the Gospels that Jesus was at times hungry:

> 'And when He had fasted forty days and forty nights, afterward He was hungry.' (Matthew 4:2)

There were times when He was thirsty, asking the woman at the well for a drink:

> 'A woman of Samaria came to draw water. Jesus said to her, "Give Me a drink." (John 4:17)

He was sometimes also very tired and needed, like every other human being, to go to sleep:

> 'But He was in the stern, asleep on a pillow.' (Mark 4:38)

Matthew and Luke also record that Jesus was tempted, like every other human being, by the devil, who tried to persuade Him off his pre-determined course, to worship and serve him (Satan). The writer to the Hebrews states very importantly:

> 'For we do not have a High Priest who cannot sympathise with our weakness, but was in all points tempted as we are, yet without sin.' (Hebrews 4:15)

In the account of Jesus' trial and eventual scourging, it is apparent that Jesus, when whipped with leaden thongs, bled like any other human being would, and when on the cross, needed a drink of vinegar to sustain him:

> 'Jesus, knowing that all things were now accomplished, that the Scripture might be fulfilled, said, "I thirst!" Now a vessel full of sour wine was sitting there; and they filled a sponge with sour wine, and put it on hyssop, and put it to His mouth.' (John19:28-29)

Jesus eventually died, as recorded in all the Gospels, especially in John Chapter 19, and was buried in a tomb like any other dead human being. So, the Nicene Creed states that He was conceived of the Holy Spirit, and born of the Virgin Mary, and <u>became Man</u>, that He suffered under Pontius Pilate, was crucified, dead, and buried.

St Paul in his letter to the Philippian church states about Jesus:

> 'Who, being in the form of God, did not consider it robbery to be equal with God, but made Himself of no reputation, taking the form of a bondservant, and coming in the likeness of men.' (Philippians 2:6-7)

So, we see that the Biblical record does not hesitate to describe Jesus as a Man. The Gospels also set out that Jesus caused real scandal amongst His hearers by word and action, by claiming to be equal with God. He said in John's Gospel, speaking to Philip the disciple,

> "Have I been with you so long, and yet you have not known Me, Philip? He who has seen Me has seen the Father also; and from now on you know Him and have seen Him" (John 14:9)

Also, in that Gospel it is recorded that Jesus said,

> "I and My Father are one." (John 10:30)

It is apparent also that He claimed to be able to forgive sins, which astounded His hearers because they said none could forgive sins except God (see His healing of the paralysed man, Mark 2:1-12, showing that He could forgive sins which resulted in the man's healing when the infirmity had apparently been caused by sin). He also performed many supernatural miracles, turning water into wine, and feeding five thousand people with five barley loaves and two small fish (see John chapter 6). In a remarkable incident when He and His disciples were in a boat on the Sea of Galilee, He stilled the storm that was threatening to drown them, speaking a word commanding the sea to be still. This caused the disciples to wonder who this man really was:

> 'Then He arose and rebuked the wind, and said to the sea, "Peace, be still!" And the wind ceased and there was a great calm. But He said to them, "Why are you so fearful? How is it that you have no faith?" And they feared exceedingly, and said to one another, "Who can this be, that even the wind and the sea obey him!" (Mark 4:39-41)

We must add to this the account of Jesus claiming to be God in themes in which He used the words "I AM", meaning by these words that He was claiming to be God. He said:

> "I AM the bread of life. He who comes to Me shall never hunger, and he who believes in Me shall never thirst." (John 6:35)

> "I AM the light of the world. He who follows Me shall not walk in darkness but have the light of life." (John 8:12)

> "Most assuredly, I say to you, before Abraham was, I AM". (John 8:58)

"I am the door. If anyone enters by Me, he will be saved, and will go in and out and find pasture." (John 10:9)

"I AM the good shepherd. The good shepherd gives His life for the sheep." (John 10:11)

"I AM the resurrection and the life. He who believes in Me, though he may die, he shall live." (John 11:25)

"I AM the way, the truth, and the life. No one comes to the Father except through Me". (John 14:6)

Despite His often foretelling His resurrection from the dead, it is apparent from the apostles' recording of this supreme miracle, that the disciples did not expect this to happen, and that the women and the disciples were amazed at this event when, after being crucified, Jesus appeared to them in a miraculous way, eventually when they were in the room and the doors were shut for fear of the Jews. So again, the Nicene Creed, after stating that He was crucified, dead, and buried, that He descended also into hell, states that on the third day He rose again from the dead and appeared to the disciples. Paul, when writing to the Christians at Corinth, says,

> 'For I delivered to you first of all that which I also received: that Christ died for our sins according to the Scriptures, and that He was buried, and that He rose again the third day according to the Scriptures, and that He was seen by Cephas, then by the twelve. After that He was seen by over five hundred brethren at once, of whom the greater part remain

to the present, but some have fallen asleep. After that He was seen by James, then by all the apostles. Then last of all He was seen by me also, as by one born out of due time.' (1 Corinthians 15:3-8)

The Nicene Creed assertion that Christ was crucified under Pontius Pilate, means that Pontius Pilate's name is being repeated every time Christians recite this Creed, placing the ministry of Jesus as a definite historical fact. The history of the Roman Empire for instance, as recorded by Flavius Josephus in his book 'Antiquities of the Jews', places the ministry of Jesus, as recorded in that work, as a definite historical fact. Luke, also an historian, of course lacking a date as we know it in our calendar, recorded the ministry of Jesus by stating other important persons known to us in secular histories:

> 'Now in the fifteenth year of the reign of Tiberius Caesar, Pontius Pilate being governor of Judea, Herod being tetrarch of Galilee, his brother Philip tetrarch of Iturea and the region of Trachonitis, and Lysanias tetrarch of Abilene, while Annas and Caiaphas were high priests, the word of God came to John the son of Zacharias in the wilderness.' (Luke 3:1-2)

These were historical people who were present on the earth at the same time as Jesus, and known to us from historical records, and proof of the fact that the records of Jesus are not any once-upon-a-time tale, but a definite and precise fact of history and to be believed as such. The History of the Roman Empire by Edward Gibbons (1776) also covers the period 27BC - 476AD, confirming the existence of these people at that time.

So, we turn to the accounts, again historical facts, in which Jesus made clear that in Him God become Man in His life, because He was God. We could also say that He was Yahweh Rapha (The Lord who heals you), and we will see that this was all about God's work of the healing of individuals and the whole of Mankind and Creation.

It is also noteworthy that Jesus, in alluding to Himself, often called Himself the Son of Man, so emphasising the fact that He belonged to Mankind:

> "For as the lightning comes from the east and flashes to the west, so also will the coming of the Son of Man be." (Matthew 24:27)

> "For whoever is ashamed of Me and My words in this adulterous and sinful generation, of him the Son of Man also will be ashamed when He comes in the glory of His Father with the holy angels." (Mark 8:38)

> "Then they will see the Son of Man coming in the clouds with great power and glory." (Mark 13:26)

> "I am. And you will see the Son of Man sitting at the right hand of the Power and coming with the clouds of heaven." (Mark 14:62)

> "For as the lightening that flashes out of one part under heaven shines to the other part under heaven, so also the Son of Man will be in His day." (Luke 17:24)

Jesus also called Himself the Son of God and confirmed His identity under oath:

> "Most assuredly, I say to you, the hour is coming, and now is, when the dead will hear the voice of the Son of God; and those who hear will live." (John 5:25)

> "If He called them gods, to whom the word of God came (and the Scripture cannot be broken) do you say of Him whom the Father sanctified and sent into the world, 'You are blaspheming.' Because I said, 'I am the Son of God?" (John 10:35-6)

> "This sickness is not unto death, but for the glory of God, that the Son of God may be glorified through it." (John 11:4)

> 'And the high priest answered and said to Him, "I put You under oath by the living God: Tell us if You are the Christ, the Son of God!" Jesus said to him, "It is as you said." (Matthew 26:63-4)

By these statements, Jesus was emphasising the fact that He was also divine. So, all these factors underline the truth of what I have described as the Incarnation. It is also worth mentioning that Jesus, in the Gospel of John, states of the Incarnation:

> "For God did not send His Son into the world to condemn the world, but that the world through Him might be saved." (John 3:17)

A more modern statement is to be found for instance, in the hymn by Cardinal Henry Newman (1865):

> Praise to the Holiest in the height,
> And in the depth be praise;

In all His words most wonderful,
Most sure in all His ways.

O loving wisdom of our God!
When all was sin and shame,
A second Adam to the fight
And to the rescue came.

From all these accounts, we see that the Incarnation is not just a theological idea but a definite statement of truth; that Jehovah (Yahweh) became man and so was both God and Man in one Person, and that this was definitely a historical event, and at a definite historical time, and at a definite historical place. We now turn to see, whilst not examining every little bit of the life of Jesus - which as John states could fill many books, the life and ministry of Jesus Christ, our Saviour from Sin, and so encompassing the healing of men both corporate and individuals, in the WHOLENESS OF BODY, MIND, AND SPIRIT.

Chapter 10 – The Life and Ministry of Jesus Christ

According to the Gospels, Jesus emerged from obscurity in the town of Nazareth where maybe He worked as a carpenter with his earthly father Joseph. He began His public ministry being heralded by a man who was called John the Baptist, who calls Him the Lamb of God:

> 'The next day John saw Jesus coming toward him, and said, "Behold! The Lamb of God who takes away the sin of the world!" (John 1:29)

This happened on the banks of the river Jordan (still so named), where crowds of people gathered to repent of their sins and to start a new life after being baptised by the prophetic figure of John. This man's place in Biblical history is described by the Apostle John in which he also refers to Jesus as the Light:

> 'There was a man sent from God, whose name was John. This man came for a witness, to bear witness of the Light, that all through him might believe. He was not that Light but was sent to bear witness of that Light. That was the true Light which gives light to every man coming into the world.' (John 1:6-9)

In the dramatic account by John, describing Jesus as the Lamb of God who takes away the sins of the world, we see the beginning of the work of Jesus as our Saviour. The description of Jesus as Lamb of God bears with it a description of the eventual sacrifice of Jesus for our sins as it implied a connection between the life of Jesus and the sacrificial lambs of the Jewish Passover Feast.

We next see Jesus calling men out of the crowd; men who became His disciples, beginning with the choice of four fishermen named Peter, Andrew, James, and John, after He had wrought the miraculous catch of fish (see Luke 5:1-11). The sight of a Rabbi calling some men to be close to Him, to be taught by Him, was common in Jesus' day. Jesus Himself was often called Rabbi, probably because He dressed in a cloak as one of them and had disciples (the Greek word translated 'disciple' is 'mathitis', which can also mean pupil, learner, or scholar). When he was introduced to Jesus, Nathanael called Him Rabbi:

> 'And Nathanael answered and said to Him, "Rabbi, You are the Son of God! You are the King of Israel!"' (John 1:49)

Sometimes the word Rabbi is altered to the word Teacher which means the same thing:

> 'Then Jesus turned, and seeing them following, said to them, "What do you seek?" They said to Him, "Rabbi" (which is to say, when translated, Teacher), "where are You staying?"' (John 1:38)

> 'Now a certain ruler asked Him, saying, "Good Teacher, what shall I do to inherit eternal life?"' (Luke 18:18)

It is apparent that Jesus eventually chose twelve disciples:

> 'And He went up on the mountain and called to Him those He Himself wanted. And they came to Him. Then He appointed twelve, that they might be with Him and that He might send them out to preach, and to have power to heal sicknesses and to cast

out demons: Simon, to whom He gave the name Peter; James the son of Zebedee and John the brother of James, to whom He gave the name Boanerges, that is, "Sons of Thunder"; Andrew, Philip, Bartholomew, Matthew, Thomas, James the son of Alphaeus, Thaddaeus, Simon the Cananite; and Judas Iscariot, who also betrayed Him.' (Mark 3:13-19)

Jesus certainly gathered the disciples around Him to be learners. His teaching is set forth in what is called The Sermon on the Mount (see Matthew chapters 5-7) during which Jesus amazes His disciples by saying, 'you have heard it was said that Moses said to you… but I say unto you ….' (See for example Matthew 5:21-22). This teaching epitomised the constant efforts of Jesus to steer His disciples away from the letter of the Law and to emphasise the spirit of the Law; to emphasise what went on in the inner life and disposition of His hearers.

These disciples, eventually numbering seventy, were not only called by Jesus to be hearers of His words, but also to be, as it were, the first missionaries sent out by Him with these words of command to them:

> "And as you go, preach, saying, 'The kingdom of heaven is at hand.' Heal the sick, cleanse the lepers, raise the dead, cast out demons. Freely you have received, freely give." (Matthew 10:7-8)

So, we see again that the healing of the whole person was the paramount teaching of the message of Jesus about the Kingdom of God. This assertion of the healing of the whole person to be God's saving work is seen again in the account of where Jesus went into the synagogue of His hometown of Nazareth, obviously as a well-known Rabbi, and stated that His own work and ministry were to be the fulfilment of the prophecy that He read out from Isaiah 61:1-2:

> "The Spirit of the Lord God is upon Me, because the Lord has anointed Me to preach good tidings to the poor; He has sent Me to heal the broken-hearted, to proclaim liberty to the captives, and the opening of the prison to those who are bound; to proclaim the acceptable year of the Lord, and the day of vengeance of our God."

Jesus astounded His hearers by saying,

> "Today this Scripture is fulfilled in your hearing." (Luke 4:21)

Again, we see the healing of the whole person being the paramount work of God's Saving Grace. It is also very apparent from the Gospels that Jesus frequently ministered to heal the sicknesses and infirmities of crowds of people:

> 'The report went around concerning Him all the more; and great multitudes came together to hear, and to be healed by Him of their infirmities.' (Luke 5:15)

It is also apparent that He ministered to individuals on their own, including a man born blind (see John 9:1-12), and the man who was paralysed from the waist down at the Pool of Bethesda (see John 5:1-16). There are in fact forty-one specific accounts of Jesus' healing work in the

Gospels. Jesus was said to be the image of the invisible God, and the Godhead in bodily form; on Earth to do the will of God:

> 'He is the image of the invisible God, the firstborn over all creation.' (Colossians 1:15)
>
> 'For in Him dwells all the fulness of the Godhead bodily.' (Colossians 2:9)
>
> "For I have come down from heaven, not to do My own will, but the will of Him who sent Me." (John 6:38)

Again, we see God as Jehovah (Yahweh) Rapha, accomplishing His healing work; we see salvation and the healing of the whole person. As mentioned above, Jesus also came to deliver people from demonic forces, often called demons or unclean spirits, that could cause insanity in the mind of those who were so demonised, for example, the man of Gadarene (See Mark 5:1-20), and also caused physical infirmities, such as causing a person to be deaf and dumb (see Mark 7:31-37), and also on at least one occasion, inflicting a young boy with what we would today call epilepsy:

> 'Suddenly a man from the multitude cried out, saying, "Teacher, I implore You, look on my son, for he is my only child. And behold, a spirit seizes him so that he foams at the mouth; and it departs from him with great difficulty, bruising him. So, I implored Your disciples to cast it out, but they could not." Then Jesus answered and said, "O faithless and perverse generation, how long shall I be with

you and bear with you? Bring your son here." And as he was still coming, the demon threw him down and convulsed him. Then Jesus rebuked the unclean spirit, healed the child, and gave him back to his father.' (Luke 9:38-42)

Finally, on occasions, Jesus portrayed His power over death even while He was on earth, raising to life for instance, in the city of Nain, the widow's only son, whilst the widow, with her mourners, were actually going to the dead young man's funeral, (see Luke 7:11-17), and also raising His friend Lazarus from the dead after he had been placed in the tomb four days earlier (see John chapter 11). In all these events and ministries Jesus was fulfilling the ministry for which He had been Incarnate, Yahweh Rapha's Saving Work, that is the complete healing of the whole person of disease, infirmity, and the ultimate end of death.

Chapter 11 – The Road to Calvary

In this chapter of the book, I will be showing that the endemic disease of sin, initially brought into the world at the fall of Adam, the first man, and perpetuated even in the modern world, was, and is, a drastic disease for which Yahweh Rapha would invoke a drastic remedy.

We have seen in the previous chapter that the saving work of Jesus was the healing of the whole person, of every individual human being personally, and of corporate humanity together. We have seen in the foregoing chapter that this work was to be salvation from sin itself, which was, and is, the basis of all humanity's problems from time immemorial to the present day. It is sin, which in itself, brought to the human body sickness, terrible problems of mental health, infestation by demonic forces, and in the end death itself, for every individual person born on the Earth. We now see that although the portrayal of the saving work in the ministry of Jesus was costly to Him, obviously in time and energy, it would, in the end, involve His actual suffering and death. This is often called GOD'S PLAN OF SALVATION.

In His ministry, Jesus was often acknowledged as, or believed to be the Messiah (meaning the Anointed One). The Jews were looking forward to His coming, to set them free from the hated Roman rule by supernatural feats of conquest, and so establishing the Jewish nation as the supreme nation on Earth. This is seen to be the belief even in the conversation that Jesus had with two disciples on the road to Emmaus. They expressed their perplexity by saying of the Jesus they thought to be dead:

> "But we were hoping that it was He who was going to redeem Israel." (Luke 24:21).

Jesus seemed at times to embrace this description of Himself as Messiah but knew that the act of salvation accomplished by the Messiah would not be in the form of conquest of the Romans but would involve His own terrible suffering and death. All this is dramatically portrayed in a scene described by Matthew, Mark, and Luke as taking place on the journey of Jesus with His disciples to a town called Caesarea Philippi. Jesus had, at this time, been with His disciples for, we approximate, eighteen months. They had heard His wondrous teaching, seen His deliverance of people from demons, and His marvellous miracles such as the feeding of five thousand people with five barley loaves and two small fish. Now, at this particular time, on this particular road, Jesus seemed to have reached a crisis moment in what His disciples understood Him, and their mission, to be. At a moment chosen by Jesus, He said to His disciples:

> "Who do men say that I, the Son of Man, am?" (Matthew 16:13)

The disciples answered Him saying,

> "Some say John the Baptist, some Elijah, and others Jeremiah or one of the prophets." (Matthew 16:14)

Jesus dismissed these answers as not true of Him and then went on to make a dramatic challenge to His disciples asking the question,

"But who do you say that I am?" (Matthew 16:15)

Peter, speaking for all the disciples said,

"You are the Christ, the Son of the living God." (Matthew 16:16)

We read in Matthew's Gospel that it was at this time that Jesus began to teach His disciples what His mission to Jerusalem would entail:

'From that time Jesus began to show His disciples that He must go to Jerusalem and suffer many things from the elders and chief priests and scribes, and be killed, and be raised the third day.' (Matthew 16:21)

With some horror, thinking of the Jewish perception of what the Messiah would be and do, Peter said to Him,

"Far be it from You, Lord; this shall not happen to You!" (Matthew 16:22)

Jesus rebuked Him saying,

"Get behind Me, Satan! You are an offence to Me, for you are not mindful of the things of God, but the things of men." (Matthew 16:23)

So, Jesus with His disciples, the disciples probably suffering from confusion, set out with determination to go to Jerusalem as told by Luke and prophesied in Isaiah:

'Now it came to pass, when the time had come for Him to be received up, that He steadfastly set His face to go to Jerusalem.' (Luke 9:51)

"For the Lord God will help Me; therefore, I will not be disgraced; therefore, I have set My face like a flint, and I will not be ashamed." (Isaiah 50:7)

Thus, Jesus fulfilled completely the 'love that drew salvation's plan' (see the words from the hymn below). This act of Jesus would encompass not only taking away the sin of the whole world but also defeating the devil on his own ground - the Earth, and importantly, having a cosmic effect reaching to the highest heaven and the lowest earth.

> Years I spent in vanity and pride,
> Caring not my Lord was crucified,
> Knowing not it was for me He died on Calvary.
>
> Mercy there was great, and grace was free,
> Pardon there was multiplied to me,
> There my burdened soul found liberty at Calvary.
>
> By God's words my last sin I learned
> Then I tremble at the Law I'd spurned,
> Till my guilty soul imploring turned to Calvary.
>
> O the love that drew salvation's plan!
> O the grace that brought it down to man!
> O the mighty gulf that God did span at Calvary.
>
> William Reed Newell (1895)

Chapter 12 – The Immortal Dies

We must see that Jesus set out to fulfil this plan to the uttermost, so throughout His life on earth He was in complete command of every detail of events that took place, exhibiting a wonderful authority in and over every situation and circumstance. People were astonished by His authority:

> "And they were astonished at His teaching, for He taught them as one having authority, and not as the scribes." (Mark 1:22)

> 'But Jesus rebuked him, saying, "Be quiet, and come out of him!" And when the unclean spirit had convulsed him and cried out with a loud voice, he came out of him. Then they were all amazed, so that they questioned among themselves, saying, "What is this? What new doctrine is this? For with authority, He commands even the unclean spirits, and they obey Him." (Mark 1:25-27).

It was this authority that marked Him out as above normal people and it was still with this authority in His Person as He fulfilled the predetermined plan of God, that He went to Jerusalem, choosing deliberately to be there when the city would be crowded with worshippers keeping the Feast of the Passover (see Matthew chapter 26).

So, for this wonderful plan of God for our Salvation to be completed, Jesus had to teach His disciples a new concept of what it meant for Him to be the Messiah - A SUFFERING MESSIAH. Again, in being a suffering Messiah, Jesus was the opposite kind of Messiah that the people of this time envisaged, and who would not entertain as such; something completely unanticipated in prophecy for the Jewish people. The perfect prophecy about the Messiah who would suffer death is to be found in what we call Isaiah Chapter 52:13 to the end of Chapter 53:

> 'Behold, My Servant shall deal prudently;
> He shall be exalted and extolled and be very high.
> Just as many were astonished at you,
> So His visage was marred more than any man,
> And His form more than the sons of men;
> So shall He sprinkle many nations.
> Kings shall shut their mouths at Him;
> For what had not been told then they shall see,
> And what they had not heard they shall consider.
>
> Who has believed our report?
> And to whom has the arm of the Lord been revealed?
> For He shall grow up before Him as a tender plant,
> And as a root out of dry ground.
> He has no form or comeliness;
> And when we see Him.,
> There is no beauty that we should desire Him.
> He is despised and rejected by men,
> A Man of sorrows and acquainted with grief.
> And we hid, as it were, our faces from Him;
> He was despised, and we did not esteem Him.
>
> Surely He has borne our griefs
> And carried our sorrows;
> Yet we esteemed Him stricken,

Smitten by God and afflicted.
But He was wounded for our transgressions,
He was bruised for our iniquities;
The chastisement for our peace was upon Him,
And by His stripes we are healed.
All we all like sheep have gone astray;
We have turned, every one, to his own way;
And the Lord has laid on Him the iniquity of us all.

He was oppressed and He was afflicted,
Yet He opened not His mouth;
He was led as a lamb to the slaughter,
And as a sheep before its shearers is silent,
So he opened not His mouth.
He was taken from prison and from judgement,
And who will declare His generation?
For He was cut off from the land of the living;
For the transgressions of My people He was stricken.
And they made His grave with the wicked -
But with the rich at His death,
Because He had done no violence,
Nor was any deceit in His mouth.

Yet it pleased the Lord to bruise Him;
He has put Him to grief.
When You make His soul an offering for sin,
He shall see His seed, He shall prolong His days,
And the pleasure of the Lord shall prosper in His hand.
He shall see the labour of His soul, and be satisfied.
By His knowledge My righteous Servant shall justify many,

> For He shall bear their iniquities.
> Therefore I will divide Him a portion with the great,
> And He shall divide the spoil with the strong,
> Because He poured out His soul unto death,
> And He was numbered with the transgressors,
> And He bore the sin of many,
> And made intercession for the transgressors.'

This prophecy was obviously in Jesus' mind for all the time of His ministry on Earth, so He said,

> "For the Son of Man has come to seek and to save that which was lost" (Luke 19:10).
>
> "For even the Son of Man did not come to be served, but to serve, and to give His life a ransom for many." (Mark 10:45)

The prophecy from Isaiah fills out the meaning of Jesus' words much further, for it states:

> 'And the Lord has laid on Him the iniquity of us all.' (Isaiah 53:6)
>
> 'He bore the sin of many and made intercession for the transgressors.' (Isaiah 53:12).

These sayings allude to what we call the 'Sin offering' of the Jewish sacrificial system as it is set out in the book of Leviticus:

> 'If he brings a lamb as his sin offering, he shall bring a female without blemish. Then he shall lay his hand on the head of the sin offering and kill it as a sin offering at the place where they kill the burnt

offering. The priest shall take some of the blood of the sin offering with his finger, put it on the horns of the altar of burnt offering, and pour all the remaining blood at the base of the altar. He shall remove all its fat, as the fat of the lamb is removed from the sacrifice of the peace offering. Then the priest shall burn it on the altar, according to the offerings made by fire to the Lord. So the priest shall make atonement for his sin that he has committed, and it shall be forgiven him.' (Leviticus 4:32-35)

It also alludes to what is called the Day of Atonement (Leviticus 16), the most sacred day ever, enacted every year by the Jewish High Priest who, after making a sacrifice for his own sins, and after many ablutions and preparations, wore a special dress, the hem of which is surrounded by tiny bells, and went into what is called the Temple's 'Holy of Holies' or 'Most Holy' (Exodus 26:33) and sprinkled the blood of a lamb on what was called 'The Mercy Seat', a slab of gold that covered the Ark of the Covenant (Exodus 25:17), where it was envisaged that God dwelt. Having sprinkled this blood, for the sins of the whole people, the High Priest rushed out to the worshippers having obtained from God complete forgiveness of all the sins of the Jewish people. This act of the High Priest entailed him going 'through the veil' - a heavy curtain that separated him and all Jews from the Presence of God (Exodus 26:31-33). This was such an auspicious occasion that a rope was tied around the High Priest as he entered within the veil, so that if he died in the process, he could be pulled out of the Presence of God without anyone going into the Holy of Holies to rescue him.

So, we see in all this that the great plan of God for man's salvation entails His chosen servant (Messiah), not only in suffering, but what was envisaged as a sacrificial death. We see that Jesus, knowingly as Son of God, went of His own volition and His own authority, deliberately to fulfil the sin offering and the work of the Day of Atonement (see Hebrews 10:1-10) for all the sins, not just of the Jewish people but of the whole of mankind, past, present, and future. So, in accordance with these inspired words, Jesus went with His disciples to Jerusalem, choosing this time when the Passover lambs would be slain, and their blood sprinkled on the doorposts of Jewish houses, remembering every year the time when God, through this act, set the enslaved Jewish people free from their Egyptian masters. Again, it is worth noting that in going to Jerusalem it is said Jesus went as an 'Exodus for His people'.

> "I am the Lord your God, who brought you out of the land of Egypt, out of the house of bondage." (Exodus 20:2)

In going of His own free will, knowing that He was going to die for the sins of the world, Jesus said,

> "For I have come down from heaven, not to do My own will, but the will of Him who sent Me." (John 6:38).

The will of God, as we have seen, involved the death of His Son as absolutely essential to what I have called 'God's Plan of Salvation'. I can imagine as Jesus stepped out of the gates of heaven saying to the Father, "What if this plan fails?" To which the Father replied, "I have no other plan."

We must understand that Jesus obviously knew precisely what was going to happen to Him at Jerusalem and so He went, not with any foreboding, despair, or negative emotion to Jerusalem, but He went boldly to His predetermined end with, as it were, His head held high, His shoulders back and, as I have said, His face set like a flint. It is important to understand that although this is foretold in Isaiah 53:3 with the words,

> 'A man of sorrows and acquainted with grief.'

He was in fact in complete charge, with His own divine authority over everything that the chief priests, and even Pontius Pilate did to Him, including His crucifixion.

A wonderful prophetic description of Jesus' crucifixion is to be read in Psalm 22:

> 'My God, My God, why have You forsaken Me?
> Why are You so far from helping Me,
> And from the words of My groaning?
> O My God, I cry in the daytime, but You do not hear;
> And in the night season, and am not silent.
>
> But You are holy,
> Enthroned in the praises of Israel.
> Our fathers trusted in You;
> They trusted, and You delivered them.
> They cried to You, and were delivered;
> They trusted in You, and were not ashamed.
>
> But I am a worm , and no man;
> A reproach of men, and despised by the people.

All those who see Me ridicule Me;
They shoot out their lip, they shake their head, saying,
"He trusted in the Lord, let Him rescue Him;
Let Him deliver Him, since He delights in Him!"

But You are He who took Me out of the womb;
You made Me trust while on My mother's breasts.
I was cast upon You from birth.
From My mother's womb You have been My God.
Be not far from Me,
For trouble is near;
For there is none to help.

Many bulls have surrounded Me;
Strong bulls of Bashan have encircled Me.
They gape at Me with their mouths,
like a raging and roaring lion.

I am poured out like water,
And all my bones are out of joint;
My heart is like wax;
It has melted within Me.
My strength is dried up like a potsherd,
and My tongue clings to My jaws;
You have brought Me to the dust of death.

For dogs have surrounded Me;
The congregation of the wicked has enclosed Me.
They pierced My hands and My feet;
I can count all my bones.
They look and stare at Me.
They divide My garments among them,

And for My clothing they cast lots.

But You, O Lord, do not be far from Me;
O My Strength, hasten to help Me!
Deliver Me from the sword,
My precious life from the power of the dog.
Save Me from the lion's mouth
And from the horns of the wild oxen!

You have answered Me.

I will declare Your name to My brethren;
In the midst of the assembly I will praise You.
You who fear the Lord, praise Him!
All you descendants of Jacob, glorify Him,
And fear Him, all you offspring of Israel!
For He has not despised nor abhorred the affliction of the afflicted;
Nor has He hidden His face from Him;
But when He cried to Him, He heard.

My praise shall be of You in the great assembly;
I will pay my vows before those who fear Him.
The poor shall eat and be satisfied;
Those who seek Him will praise the Lord.
Let your heart live forever!

All the ends of the world shall remember and turn to the Lord,
And all the families of the nations shall worship before You!
For the kingdom is the Lord's, and He rules over the nations.

All the prosperous of the earth shall eat and worship;
All those who go down to the dust shall bow before Him,
Even he who cannot keep himself alive.

A posterity shall serve Him.
It will be recounted of the Lord to the next generation,
They will come and declare His righteousness to a people who will be born,
That He has done this.

We can further discover what Jesus' Crucifixion meant to His Father and Himself as a drastic remedy for sin when we read Jesus' words on the cross in which He quotes directly from Psalm 22:

> "My God, My God, why have You forsaken Me?" (Mark 15:34)

Sin, as we see, results in the separation of Man from God, and as Jesus Himself was a sinless sacrifice, we can see that His experience of being separated from God was as in the words of Peter:

> 'who Himself bore our sins in His own body on the tree, that we, having died to sins, might live for righteousness – by whose stripes you were healed.' (1Peter 2:24)

And we have Isaiah's prediction that God laid on Him the sin of the whole world, and of all this dramatic event, of which Paul said,

> 'God was in Christ reconciling the world to Himself, not imputing their trespasses to them, and has committed to us the word of reconciliation.' (2 Corinthians 5:19)

The further, and very important, truth is expounded when Jesus declared,

> "It is finished!" (John 19:30)

In the Greek, this phrase really means as well: It is completed, perfected, absolutely done, so that nothing whatsoever could be needed to add or detract from this absolutely finished remedy and plan of God for the salvation of humanity, reversing entirely the dreadful results of man's Fall in the sin of Adam.

> 'For He made Him who knew no sin to be sin for us, that we might become the righteousness of God in Him.' (2 Corinthians 5:21)

The perfect sacrifice had been made. It had been completed according to God's holy plan, the fulfilment of all the laws of sacrifice; the ultimate sacrificial love to purchase the Salvation of mankind.

> Man of Sorrows! What a name
> For the Son of God, who came
> Ruined sinners to reclaim;
> Hallelujah! What a Saviour!

Bearing shame and scoffing rude,
In my place condemned He stood;
Sealed my pardon with His blood;
Hallelujah! What a Saviour!

Guilty, vile, and helpless we;
Spotless Lamb of God was He;
Full atonement! Can it be?
Hallelujah! What a Saviour!

Lifted up was He to die;
It is finished! Was His cry;
Now in Heaven exalted high;
Hallelujah! What a Saviour!

When He comes, our glorious King,
All His ransomed home to bring,
Then anew His song we'll sing:
Hallelujah! What a Saviour!
                    P.P. Bliss (1875)

I have taught that Jesus was in complete control of everything that happened to Him after He appealed to His Father in the Garden of Gethsemane:

> "Father, if it is Your will, take this cup away from Me; nevertheless, not My will, but Yours, be done." (Luke 22:42)

This applies even to the very moment when He actually died that we read in Matthew 27:50:

> 'And Jesus cried out again with a loud voice and yielded up His spirit.'

The fact that the word used here, translated from the Greek, is yielded, means that Jesus did this, at the precise moment, of His own choice, so that by His own will and act He deliberately gave up His spirit and died.

This is again borne out by the fact that when soldiers went to break the legs of the three crucified people, so that they would not hang on a cross for the preparation for the Passover, it is recorded that they did break the legs of the two criminals crucified with Jesus, but they surprisingly found that Jesus was already dead and so had no reason to.

> 'But when they came to Jesus and saw that He was already dead, they did not break His legs.' (John 19:33)

It is very important also to understand that a very dramatic, magnificent, and supernatural event took place as Jesus, quoting from Psalm 31:5, said on the cross His last words:

> "Father, into Your hands I commit My Spirit." (Luke 23:46).

At the very moment He said these words it is recorded that the heavy veil, that separated ordinary humanity from the presence of God was dramatically torn in two:

> 'Then, behold, the veil of the temple was torn in two from top to bottom; and the earth quaked, and the rocks were split.' (Matthew 27:51)

By this God, that is Father, Son, and Holy Spirit, signifies that now, because of Jesus' perfect sacrifice on the Cross, the way was now open for any human being who believed in this act to enter without let or hindrance into the Shekinah Glory of God's Presence to commune with Him.

> 'By that will we have been sanctified through the offering of the body of Jesus Christ once for all.' (Hebrews 10:10)

This sanctification through the offering of the body of Jesus Christ that tore the veil from between humans and God their Father is dramatically caught up in the words of Charles Wesley (1738):

> And can it be that I should gain
> An int'rest in the Saviour's blood?
> Died He for me, who caused His pain?
> For me, who Him to death pursued?
> Amazing love! How can it be,
> That Thou, my God, shouldst die for me?
>
> 'Tis myst'ry all! Th' Immortal dies!
> Who can explore His strange design?
> In vain the firstborn seraph tries
> To sound the depths of love divine.
> 'Tis mercy all! Let earth adore,
> Let angel minds inquire no more.
>
> He left His Father's throne above,
> So free, so infinite His Grace;
> Emptied Himself of all but love,
> And bled for Adam's helpless race:
> 'Tis mercy all, immense and free,
> For, O my God, it found out me!

Long my imprisoned spirit lay,
Fast bound in sin and nature's night;
Thine eye diffused a quick'ning ray,
I woke, the dungeon flamed with light;
My chains fell off, my heart was free;
I rose, went forth, and followed Thee.

No condemnation now I dread;
Jesus, and all in Him is mine;
Alive in Him, my living Head,
And clothed in righteousness divine,
Bold I approach the eternal throne,
And claim the crown, through Christ my own.

So, we see God's Drastic Remedy for the Endemic Disease of Sin in human life, perfectly fulfilled and enacted in the life, suffering and death of our Lord and Saviour Jesus Christ.

Chapter 13 – The Resurrection of Jesus Christ

It is noteworthy, as we study the four Gospels about the suffering and death of our Lord Jesus Christ, that He, in fact, never foretold this dramatic remedy for sin without telling His disciples:

> "The Son of Man is being betrayed into the hands of men, and they will kill Him. And after He is killed, He will rise on the third day". (Mark 9:31)

So, as we have seen, Jesus not only foresaw His suffering and death but also, without any let or hindrance, that He would rise again on the third day after His crucifixion. We know that the concept of rising again from the dead was not a new and foreign thought to the Jewish people from the account of the raising of Lazarus, when Martha said to Jesus, when He was going to the tomb of her brother Lazarus,

> "I know that he will rise again in the resurrection at the last day." (John 11:24)

It is important to notice also, that the concept of resurrection of dead people is fundamentally different from any idea of immortality in life after death, which is believed by many religions of the world, including Islam. This fundamental truth about a resurrection of the dead is captured in the Nicene Creed which states that Christians believe in:

> 'THE RESURRECTION OF THE BODY AND LIFE EVERLASTING.'

Again, this concept differs from Hinduism and Buddhism. Although they do believe in an immortal life for every human being, they see it as a sort of drop of water lost in a vast ocean, a rather negative view of immortal life as far as Jews and Christians are concerned. The Christian belief is that the whole person - body, soul (mind), and Spirit, come into an existence, not just of immortality but of eternal life, for which Jesus prayed for us:

> "And this is eternal life, that they may know You, the only true God, and Jesus Christ whom You have sent." (John 17:3)

This eternal life is a life of a new quality and quantity, experienced by the whole person, as a recognisable being as they appeared in their finite life on earth. Thus, Christians believe, as Paul taught in 1 Corinthians 15 that:

> 'Now Christ is risen from the dead and has become the first fruits of those who have fallen asleep.' (1 Corinthians 15:20)

So again, as Paul stated, Christians believe that Jesus was the first person to be clothed with this resurrection body, that was eventually recognised as Jesus risen from the dead by, for example, Mary Magdalene, and eventually all the disciples. This teaching of Paul in 1 Corinthians 15 (a dramatic exegesis of what resurrection really envisages and means), states that the proof of the resurrection of Jesus after His crucifixion was witnessed for forty days by many believers.

> "Moreover, brethren, I declare to you the gospel which I preached to you, which also you received

and in which you stand, by which you are also saved, if you hold fast that word which I preached to you - unless you believed in vain. For I delivered to you first of all that which I also received: that Christ died for our sins according to the Scriptures, and that He was buried, and that He rose again the third day according to the Scriptures, and that He was seen by Cephas, then by the twelve. After that He was seen by over five hundred brethren at once, of whom the greater part remain to the present, but some have fallen asleep. After that He was seen by James, then by all the apostles. Then last of all He was seen by me also, as by one born out of due time." (1 Corinthians 15:1-8)

Jesus was obviously seen and recognised in His new resurrection body which could travel about in an ethereal way, not being obstructed even by walls and locked doors:

> 'Then, the same day at evening, being the first day of the week, when the doors were shut where the disciples were assembled, for fear of the Jews, Jesus came and stood in the midst, and said to them, "Peace be with you." When He had said this, He showed them His hands and His side. Then the disciples were glad when they saw the Lord.' (John 20:19-20)

Jesus could appear in a recognisable form to people on earth in their natural bodies, and was seen with their natural eyes, whenever and wherever He wanted to, even on a seashore when His disciples were fishing a distance away:

> 'Now when Simon Peter heard that it was the Lord, he put on his outer garment (for he had removed it) and plunged into the sea.' (John 21:7).

It is also apparent that the resurrected Jesus could even know the thoughts of a human being, so, for instance, He knew that Thomas doubted His resurrection and knew the conditions on which Thomas (often known as doubting Thomas) would actually believe, that is, putting his fingers into the nail prints of Jesus' hands and his hand into Jesus' side where a spear had been thrust whilst on the cross.

> "Now Thomas, called the Twin, one of the twelve, was not with them when Jesus came. The other disciples therefore said to him, "We have seen the Lord." So he said to them, "Unless I see in His hands and the print of the nails, and put my finger into the print of the nails, and put my hand into His side, I will not believe." And after eight days His disciples were again inside, and Thomas with them. Jesus came, the doors being shut, and stood in the midst, and said, "Peace to you!" Then He said to Thomas, "Reach your finger here, and look at My hands; and reach your hand here, and put it into My side. Do not be unbelieving, but believing." And Thomas answered and said to Him, "My Lord and My God!" Jesus said to him, "Thomas, because you have seen Me, you have believed. Blessed are those who have not seen and yet have believed." (John 20:24-29)

The risen Jesus, in His loving grace, fulfilled Thomas' desire in such a way that Thomas fell at Jesus' feet saying, "My Lord and My God!" All this wonderful and inspired truth about the resurrection of Jesus on the third day after

His Crucifixion overcomes the confused account, and initial disbelief of the disciples, on the discovery that the stone had been rolled away from the tomb where that, absolutely certain, dead body of Jesus had been placed, and significantly, the Bible accounts say the stone had been rolled away from the tomb. that had been provided for the body of Jesus by a secret disciple named Joseph of Arimathea. This inspired account of the Resurrection of Jesus is unique, and the Christian belief in resurrection is distinct from all other religions of the world. The Nicene Creed says of Jesus, that He suffered under Pontius Pilate, was crucified, dead, and buried, but on the third day rose again from the dead and ascended into Heaven.

The fact that Jesus rose from the dead on the first day of the week according to the inspired accounts in the Gospel, can be believed as an empirical fact by all but the most stubborn of doubters. The first Christians greeted each other on the first day of the week at Easter shouting to one another:

"THE LORD IS RISEN!"

Answer:

"HE IS RISEN INDEED!"

They were very soon to die terrible deaths by the Roman Emperor's dictates, what Christians call martyrs, rather than for one moment, and quite easily, denying this truth.

Chapter 14 – The Ascension of Jesus Christ

The word 'ascension' literally means in the Greek 'going up'. The Christian belief in the Ascension of Jesus is based on the account recorded in the Acts of the Apostles Chapter 1:9-11 as follows:

> 'Now when He had spoken these things, while they watched, He was taken up, and a cloud received Him out of their sight. And while they looked steadfastly toward heaven as He went up, behold two men stood by them in white apparel, who also said, "Men of Galilee, why do you stand gazing up into heaven? This same Jesus, who was taken up from you into heaven, will so come in like manner as you saw Him go into heaven."

To understand it fully, we must take account of the cosmology (worldview) of the people, including the Jews, of the first century AD. Their 'worldview' was of a three-storey universe, in which Heaven was up above the sky, and the Earth - which was deemed to be flat and held up by pillars - was sandwiched in the middle between Heaven and what was called Hades, that later became known as Hell. This is borne out by, for instance, Paul's words to the Philippians:

> 'Let this be in your mind which was also in Christ Jesus, who, being in the form of God, did not consider it robbery to be equal with God, but made Himself of no reputation, taking the form of a

> bondservant, and coming in the likeness of men. And being found in appearance as a man, He humbled Himself and became obedient to the point of death, even the death of the cross. Therefore, God has also highly exalted Him and given Him the name which is above every name, that at the name of Jesus every knee should bow, of those in heaven, and of those on the earth, and of those under the earth, and that every tongue should confess that Jesus Christ is Lord, to the glory of God the Father.' (Philippians 2:5-11)

These words formed part of an early Christian hymn sung every time the early Christians were at worship. So we see that as Jesus could only show them truth in a way that they could understand, He had literally to 'go up' in their sight, so they knew He would be forever with the Lord God and no longer present to their earthly senses. This truth is shown in the New Testament to have very important and significant theological implications. Paul declares that Jesus has defeated all satanic forces including heavenly princelings, demons, and spirits:

> 'He raised Him from the dead and seated Him at His right hand in the heavenly places, far above all principality and power and might and dominion, and every name that is named, not only in this age but also in that which is to come.' (Ephesians 1:20-22)

By this, Christians can have the assurance that they too can share the Lord's victory, especially by using His name as He Himself has promised, recorded in the Gospel of John.

> "Most assuredly, I say to you, whatever you ask the Father in My name He will give you. Until now you have asked nothing in My name. Ask, and you will receive, that your joy may be full." (John 16:23-24)

So, no Christian then or now has the slightest need to fear the power of any evil forces in any way, but in fact, they can drive these forces away from them to Hades by declaring the Lord's name to vindicate their action and pronouncement. Another wonderful New Testament picture about the Ascension of Jesus says that He led captivity captive through the heavenly realm, just as a Roman General would go on what was called a triumphal procession through the streets of Rome with his conquered foes trailing along behind him to the shouts and acclaim of the onlookers. In his letter to the Ephesians chapter 4:8, Paul quotes from the Psalms:

> 'You have ascended on high, You have led captivity captive; You have received gifts among men. Even from the rebellious, that the Lord God might dwell there.' (Psalm 68:18)

Further to these dramatic inspired truths, it is important also to understand the Biblical pronouncement. Again, as we have seen, and was previously shown to Thomas, Jesus bore in His Spiritual Body the marks of His crucifixion, paying the price for our salvation, eternally seen in the heavenly realm. The image of the risen body of Christ bearing His sacrificial wounds is beautifully captured in the words of Charles Wesley's hymn:

Arise, my soul, arise!
Shake off thy guilty fears;
The bleeding Sacrifice
In my behalf appears.
Before the throne my Surety stands;
My name is written on His hands.

He ever lives above,
For me to intercede,
His all-redeeming love,
His precious blood to plead.
His blood was shed for every race,
And sprinkles now the throne of grace.

Five bleeding wounds He bears,
Received on Calvary;
They pour effectual prayers
They strongly plead for me.
Forgive him, O forgive, they cry,
Nor let that ransomed sinner die!

The Father hears Him pray,
His dear anointed One;
He cannot turn away
The presence of His Son.
His spirit answers to the blood,
And tells me I am born of God.

To God I am reconciled
His pardoning voice I hear;
He owns me for His child,
I can no longer fear.
With confidence I now draw nigh,

And "Father, Abba, Father!" cry.
Charles Wesley (1742)

There are other inspired truths that follow from this simple fact of the Ascension of the Lord Jesus Christ, for instance, that in ascending to Heaven and to the Father's presence He showed in eternity that through His death, as we have seen on Earth, so in Heaven the veil separating sinful human beings from a holy God has been completely taken away, and so a Christian in his or her prayers can, in his spirit and mind as it were, enter into the very holy of holies in heaven; into their Father's Presence.

> 'Therefore, brethren, having boldness to enter the Holiest by the blood of Jesus, by a new and living way which He consecrated for us, through the veil, that is, His flesh, and having a High Priest over the house of God, let us draw near with a true heart in full assurance of faith, having our hearts sprinkled from an evil conscience and our bodies washed with pure water. Let us hold fast the confession of our hope without wavering, for He who promised is faithful.' (Hebrews 10:19-23).

So also, our complete salvation and destiny in Heaven is secured for us because our Brother has gone there before us as He told us:

> "Where I am going you cannot follow Me now, but you shall follow Me afterward." (John 13:36)

This particular inspired verse is a culmination of Jesus' discourses with His disciples at what is called the Last

Supper, where He repeatedly said to them that He was going away from them. He also said that unless He went away, what He called the Holy Spirit (Greek Paraclete) could not be sent to them to inspire them in the service He commanded them to do for Him, in what is recorded in Scripture, as His very last words:

> "Go therefore and make disciples of all nations, baptising them in the name of the Father and of the Son and of the Holy Spirit, teaching them to observe all things that I have commanded you; and lo, I am with you always, even to the end of the age." (Matthew 28:19-20)

One last thought about Jesus Christ's Ascension, but a very important one, quoted by two men in white who were present with the Risen Jesus and His disciples on the Mount of Olives at His Ascension when they said:

> "Men of Galilee, why do you stand gazing up into heaven? This same Jesus, who was taken up from you into heaven? This same Jesus, who was taken up from you into heaven, will so come in like manner as you saw Him go into heaven." (Acts 1:11).

So, these very last words spoken on Earth about Jesus' ascending from Earth to Heaven, infallibly predicted, by angels, is the glorious return at the end of time by the Risen Lord, to establish His complete Kingdom at the end of the Ages at the Lord's triumphant second coming. The victory of Christ and His Ascension are again captured in the words of a wonderful hymn:

Alleluia! Sing to Jesus!
His the sceptre, His the Throne.
Alleluia! His the triumph,
His the victory alone.
Hark! The songs of peaceful Zion
Thunder like a mighty flood:
"Jesus, out of ev'ry nation
Has redeemed us by His blood."

Alleluia! Not as orphans
Are we left in sorrow now;
Alleluia! He is near us;
Faith believes, nor questions how.
Though the cloud from sight received Him
When the forty days were o'er,
Shall our hearts forget His promise:
"I am with you evermore"?

Alleluia! Bread of angels,
Here on earth our food, our stay!
Alleluia! Here the sinful
Flee to You from day to day.
Intercessor, friend of sinners,
Earth's redeemer, plead for me,
Where the songs of all the sinless
Sweep across the crystal sea.

Alleluia! King eternal,
You the Lord of lords we own;
Alleluia! Born of Mary,
Earth Your footstool, Heav'n Your throne.
You within the veil have entered,

Robed in flesh, our great high priest;
Here on earth both priest and sacrifice,
In the eucharistic feast.

     W Chatterton Dix (1866)

PART THREE

The Power of the Blood

Chapter 15 – The Crucifixion: the 'Power of the Blood'

I have shared that the human race, from the time of Adam till now, has been suffering from an endemic disease which the Bible terms SIN. I have also shown the drastic remedy in which Yahweh Rapha had to engage in, completely and absolutely, to provide a cure for this disease at its very source. As already noted, this is sometimes termed 'God's Plan of Salvation', especially by evangelical Christians. We have seen that Jesus' words on the Cross, "It is finished!" (John 19:30), denote that nothing needs to be added to, and nothing can be taken away from, this complete act of God. We have seen that the disease of sin could in no way be cured by any human act, either corporately or individually, and indeed, because this act of God is both final and complete, we now need to see how human beings can partake of, or lay hold of, this wonderful Work of God and make it real for themselves, especially individually, and then for the salvation of the whole of humanity, and also how all this Work will, in the end, affect the whole of the realm of Nature.

We have also seen that, contrary to the Jewish expectation of the omnipotent and all-conquering Messiah, this work involved the Incarnation of God's Son, as a suffering Messiah who would appear to some to have been defeated in His purpose but, in fact, through His suffering and death, He defeated Sin and all its ensuing problems including the death of every individual person who could lay hold of this Work in a personal way. We have seen that this particular Work of Yahweh Rapha, is enshrined in the words of Jesus recorded in John's Gospel Chapter 3:16:

"God so loved the world that He gave His only begotten Son, that whoever believes in Him should not perish but have everlasting life."

To grasp and obtain the blessings of this wonderful Work we must first of all see what the Bible states in 1 John 1:7:

> 'The blood of Jesus Christ His Son cleanses us from all sin.'

The concept of Jesus' death being described as 'His Blood' is first denoted by Jesus Christ at the Last Supper with his disciples where He inaugurates the repetition of this simple meal by His disciples saying as they took the bread,

> "This is My body which is given for you; do this in remembrance of Me." (Luke 22:19)

Then when He shared a single simple cup of wine He said,

> "Drink from it all of you. For this is My blood of the new covenant, which is shed for many for the remission of sins." (Matthew 26:27-28).

The inspired words of the apostles, acknowledging that it is only the blood from a sacrifice that can atone for sins, confirms this:

> 'And according to the law almost all things are purified with blood, and without shedding of blood there can be no remission.' (Hebrews 9:22).

Because of these words of Jesus and the Apostles, and elsewhere in the New Testament, it shows how the powerful words 'His blood' have become a simple way of designating the whole sacrifice of our Lord Jesus Christ on the Cross. This is seen for instance in many hymns exemplifying this:

> There is a fountain filled with blood,
> Drawn from Immanuel's veins,
> And sinners plunged beneath that flood
> Lose all their guilty stains.
>
> The dying thief rejoiced to see
> That fountain in His day;
> And there have I, though vile as he,
> Washed all my sins away.
>
> Dear dying Lamb, Thy precious blood
> Shall never lose its pow'r,
> Till all the ransomed church of God
> Are saved, to sin no more.
>
> E'er since by faith I saw the stream
> Thy flowing wounds supply,
> Redeeming love has been my theme,
> And shall be till I die.
>
> When this poor, lisping, stamm'ring tongue
> Lies silent in the grave,
> Then in a nobler, sweeter song,
> I'll sing Thy pow'r to save.
>
> William Cowper (1772)

And:

> Now I have found the ground wherein
> Sure my soul's anchor may remain -
> The wounds of Jesus, for my sin
> Before the world's foundation slain;
> Whose mercy shall unshaken stay,
> When heav'n and earth are fled away.
>
> Father, Thine everlasting grace
> Our scanty thought surpasses far,
> Thy heart still melts with tenderness,
> Thy arms of love still open are,
> Returning sinners to receive,
> That mercy they may taste and live.
>
> O Love, Thou bottomless abyss,
> My sins are swallowed up in Thee!
> Covered is my unrighteousness,
> Nor spot of guilt remains on me,
> While Jesus' blood, through earth and skies
> Mercy, free, boundless mercy! Cries.
> > Johann Andreas Rothe (1688-1758)
> > translated by John Wesley

And:

> Glory be to Jesus,
> who in bitter pains
> poured for me the life-blood
> from His sacred veins.
>
> Grace and life eternal
> in that Blood I find;

blest be His compassion,
infinitely kind.

Blest through endless ages
be the precious stream,
which from endless torments
did the world redeem.

Abel's blood for vengeance
pleaded to the skies;
But the blood of Jesus
for our pardon cries.

It the conscience sprinkles,
frees our guilty hearts;
Satan in confusion
terror-struck departs.

Oft as earth exulting
wafts its praise on high,
angel-hosts rejoicing
make their glad reply.

Lift ye then your voices;
swell the mighty flood;
Louder still and louder
praise the precious Blood!
                    Edward Caswall (1857)

Many Christians believe that simply understanding this to be true on a rational level is sufficient to be saved. However, others, like me, believe that if this is truly embraced it will involve the emotions as well as the mind.

A prime example of this is to be found in the well-known Church of England minister named John Wesley (the founder of Methodism). In his diary it is obvious that as an ordained clergyman in the Church of England he believed all this to be true and engaged in a whole panorama of good works which he believed would help his salvation, founding what was called The Holy Club at Oxford University. However, despite all his efforts, he was not satisfied with his spiritual life. Certainly, he would remember the words of his father Samuel, also a Church of England clergyman, who kept saying to his son John, "Remember the inward witness son, remember the inward witness."

No doubt John was also influenced by the simple faith of his mother Susanna who had found her own simple peace with God without all this effort. Finally, John Wesley was also influenced by a German denomination of Christians, The Moravians, who, when in a severe storm on a boat, were in complete peace, while John was frightened. Eventually, a Moravian called Peter Bohler also had a great influence upon John Wesley which resulted in a life-transforming moment for John on the 24th of May 1738. He states in his diary for that day:

> "At a quarter before nine, when someone was reading Luther's Preface to the Epistle to the Romans, my heart was strangely warmed and I felt that I did trust in Christ alone for my salvation, and an assurance was given me that He had saved me from the Law of Sin and Death."

This was completely life transforming for John Wesley who has been called the 'Knight of the burning heart' and led to him preaching about the wonder of this experience to many under-privileged men and women in different parts of England with the result that his Methodist movement was said to change England into a 'A nest of singing birds'. True, in the conversion of a man called Francis Astbury this 'inward witness' became a dominant theme in the now increasingly vast number of people who emigrated to America. This taking hold of the Work of the Blood of Jesus has become the dominant theme in the preaching and theology of evangelical Christians of all denominations to this present day. John's brother Charles, also had this experience and became the gifted hymn writer of the Methodist movement, enshrining its theology and motivating experience, for instance in the hymn 'And can it be' already quoted in Chapter 12. This truth is enshrined in Scripture in Ephesians 2:8-9:

> 'For by grace you have been saved through faith, and that not of yourselves; it is a gift of God, not of works lest anyone should boast."

A very traumatic and visually marvellous picture of this Saving Blood is found in the Book of Revelation chapter 7:9 -17:

> 'After these things I looked, and behold, a great multitude which no one could number, of all nations, tribes, peoples, and tongues, standing before the throne and before the Lamb, clothed with white robes, with palm branches in their hands, and crying out with a loud voice, saying, "Salvation

belongs to our God who sits on the throne, and to the Lamb!" All the angels stood around the throne and the elders and the four living creatures, and fell on their faces before the throne and worshipped God saying: "Amen! Blessing and glory and wisdom, thanksgiving and honour and power and might, be to our God forever and ever. Amen!"

Then one of the elders answered, saying to me, "Who are these arrayed in white robes, and where did they come from?" And I said to him, "Sir, you know."

So he said to me, "These are the ones who come out of the great tribulation, and washed their robes and made them white in the blood of the Lamb. Therefore they are before the throne of God, and serve Him day and night in His temple. And He who sits on the throne will dwell among them. They shall neither hunger anymore nor thirst anymore; the sun shall not strike them, nor any heat; for the Lamb who is in the midst of the throne will shepherd them and lead them to living fountains of waters. And God will wipe away every tear from their eyes."

And in Revelation 5:9-13:

'And they sang a new song, saying: "You are worthy to take the scroll, and to open its seals; for You were slain, and have redeemed us to God by Your blood out of every tribe and tongue and people and nation, and have made us kings and priests to our God; and we shall reign on the earth."

Then I looked, and I heard the voice of many angels around the throne, the living creatures, and the elders; and the number of them was ten thousand times ten thousand, and thousands of thousands, saying with a loud voice:

> "Worthy is the Lamb who was slain
> To receive power and riches and wisdom,
> And strength and honour and glory and blessing!"

And every creature which is in heaven and on the earth and under the earth and such as are in the sea, and all that are in them, I heard saying:

> "Blessing and honour and glory and power
> Be to Him who sits on the throne,
> And to the Lamb, forever and ever!"

In all this we see that Jesus' death, resurrection, and ascension is efficacious for the forgiveness of all sins committed by any person who believes that this wonderful Work of God actually happened through God's Grace (Grace meaning undeserved love in action), and when that person seeking forgiveness of sins has faith in this act, to forgive all their sins.

We have seen however, in the Biblical exposition about Sin, that actual sins are indications and symptoms of a very deadly disease that brings the entire death of every human being in his or her spirit, soul and body:

> 'For since by Man came death, by Man also came the resurrection of the dead.' (1 Corinthians 15:21)

We can now see however, that the glorious Work of Christ on the Cross did not only bring about the forgiveness of sins, but also dealt a tremendous healing blow to the very nature of the disease of sin itself (sometimes called Original Sin). The New Testament in several places sets forth this truth that can even be seen in the life of a believer. So Paul, for instance, in his letter to the Romans, states emphatically for a believer that,

> 'Sin shall not have dominion over you, for you are not under law but under grace.' (Romans 6:14)

He also writes:

> 'But now having been set free from sin, and having become slaves of God, you have your fruit to holiness, and in the end, everlasting life. For the wages of sin is death, but the gift of God is eternal life in Christ Jesus our Lord.' (Romans 6:22-23).

Jesus Himself reiterated at the end of the Sermon on the Mount,

> "Therefore you shall be perfect, just as your Father in heaven is perfect." (Matthew 5:48).

Peter also exhorts Christians to whom he is writing to seek to be perfect, or holy, quoting from the command in Leviticus 11:44:

> 'As He who called you is holy, you also be holy in all your conduct, because it is written, "Be holy, for I am holy." (1 Peter 1:15-16).

The reference to those who washed their robes and made them white in the Blood of the Lamb (in Revelation quoted above) also indicates that now these worshippers in heaven are absolutely pure. Again, the New Testament indicates that at the end of time the redeemed Church of God shall be presented to Christ as a bride 'without spot or wrinkle.':

> 'Christ also loved the church and gave Himself for her, that He might sanctify and cleanse her with the washing of water by the word, that He might present her to Himself a glorious church, not having spot or wrinkle or any such thing, but that she should be holy and without blemish.' (Ephesians 5:25-27).

Peter, in his first epistle, reminds the Church that their redemption, and healing from sin, was not paid for with any earthly riches, or from observance of tradition, but only with the spotless blood of the Lamb – Jesus Christ:

> 'You were not redeemed with corruptible things, like silver or gold, from your aimless conduct received by tradition from your fathers, but with the precious blood of Christ, as of a lamb without blemish and without spot.' (1 Peter 1:18-19)

In my experience, I have found that Christians are very happy to rejoice in the assurance of the forgiveness of their sins at the beginning of their Christian lives (called by theologians 'regeneration'), but often do not go on to cooperate with God in their complete healing on Earth; of aiming for holiness (called by theologians 'sanctification' - being made holy), and I have not heard of any Christian to be without sin and be entirely holy in their present life, and I think they would not claim to be in that sublime state because they feel, quite rightly, that to claim this would infer pride of status that in itself would be a sin. Throughout Christian history however, the description of a believer who has been 'sanctified' or, as the Roman Catholic Church says, a saint, is part of their doctrine, and some evangelical Christians have stated that this can be a possibility in what are commonly called 'Holiness Movements', and John Wesley certainly believed this too, stating that the people called Methodists had been called into being to spread Scriptural Holiness throughout the land, and many of Charles Wesley's hymns also described this state as a possibility, to be attained even in a moment of time and remarkable faith. For example, a hymn (not by Charles Wesley), denoting this truth is:

> Rock of Ages, cleft for me
> let me hide myself in Thee;
> let the water and the blood,
> from Thy riven side which flowed,
> be of sin the double cure;
> cleanse me from wrath and make me pure.
>
> Nothing in my hand I bring,
> simply to Thy cross I cling;
> naked, come to Thee for dress;
> helpless, look to Thee for grace;
> vile, I to the fountain fly;
> wash me, Saviour, or I die.
>
> Augustus Toplady (1776)

So, in all this we see that God's Plan of Salvation, summarised in these words:

'The Blood of Jesus Christ His Son cleanses us from all sin.' (1John 1:7)

is an absolute and perfect healing from the sin and guilt which entered the world through Adam; a perfect healing to be seen on earth and eventually in God's final kingdom in Heaven. The sanctifying nature of God and the desire to be pure and spotless is also expressed in the hymn by Charles Wesley:

> Love Divine all loves excelling,
> Joy of Heaven to Earth come down,
> Fix in us Thy humble dwelling,
> All Thy faithful mercies crown.
> Jesus, Thou art all compassion,
> Pure, unbounded love Thou art.
> Visit us with Thy salvation.
> Enter every trembling heart.
>
> Breath, O breathe Thy loving spirit
> Into every troubled breast.
> Let us all in Thee inherit,
> Let us find the promised rest.
> Take away the love of sinning.
> Alpha and Omega be.
> End of faith, as its beginning,
> Sets our hearts at liberty.
>
> Come, Almighty, to deliver,
> Let us all Thy life receive.
> Suddenly return, and never,
> Never more Thy temples leave.
> Thee we would be always blessing,

Serve Thee as Thy hosts above,
Pray, and praise Thee without ceasing,
Glory in Thy perfect love.

Finish, then, Thy new creation,
Pure and spotless let us be.
Let us see Thy great salvation
Perfectly restored in Thee.
Changed from glory unto glory,
'Till in Heaven we take our place,
'Till we cast our crowns before Thee,
Lost in wonder, love, and praise.

Charles Wesley (1747)

Chapter 16 – The Blood and the Blessed Trinity

So far, we have seen what the Bible teaches about the way that human life and its environment, in all its completeness, fell into great distress. In Adam, we have seen that the human person as an individual became liable to sin and death through disobedience to God and this also included the sentence of death upon his wife and the incursion into nature of things like weeds and so on; things that militate against human beings seeking their utmost good in every way. As has been noted previously, Paul says that sin entered the world through Adam, and death through sin, and later in the epistle to the Romans he says the whole creation travails and suffers from then until now, waiting for the adoption of the sons of God.

So the whole of human life, individual, corporate, personal, and social, is included in this drastic result of Adam's sin coming right up to the present time, when despite all human efforts and some real achievements, especially in the medical field, the human race still is in great distress with wars, murders, death, afflictions and so on. We have seen also that God's great love for the human race did not in any way diminish in spite of the Fall, and in His grace, He knew that to set this terrible result of sin in abeyance, it would need the death of His only Son, Jesus Christ, whom we call our Messiah, and the second person of the Trinity. We have seen what it cost God the Father in Christ, to suffer at Calvary's cross, spiritually, mentally, and physically before He could say – in the Greek 'teleiose' – "It is finished"; completely perfected –

nothing could be added to it or taken from it; the only way of Salvation was perfectly finished for human beings to partake of.

Although I have emphasised Yahweh Rapha, the healing nature and activity of God, His work of Salvation, is:

1) initiated by God the Father

2) undertaken by God the Son

3) effected by God the Holy Spirit

and therefore, is a work of the whole of the Blessed Trinity.

As stated, in Paul's second epistle to Timothy, all Scripture must be acknowledged as God-breathed.

> 'You must continue in the things which you have learned and been assured of, knowing from whom you learned them, and that from childhood you have known the Holy Scriptures, which are able to make you wise for salvation through faith which is in Christ Jesus. All Scripture is given by inspiration of God, and is profitable for doctrine, for reproof, for correction, for instruction in righteousness, that the man of God may be complete, thoroughly equipped for every good work.' (2 Timothy 3:14-17)

If Scriptural statements such as those recounting the great acts of Salvation and Revelation are God breathed, they are therefore infallible; so also infallible is the description of the causes of the human tragedy of sin, and God's act of healing this cosmic chasm, that is the separation from God, and the recreation of nature. This is summarised by Paul in his letter to the Romans:

> 'There is therefore no condemnation to those who are in Christ Jesus, who do not walk according to the flesh, but according to the Spirit. For the law of the Spirit of life in Christ Jesus has made me free from the law of sin and death. For what the law could not do in that it was weak through the flesh, God did by sending His own Son in the likeness of sinful flesh, on account of sin; He condemned sin in the flesh, that the righteous requirement of the law might be fulfilled in us who do not walk according to the flesh but according to the Spirit.' (Romans 8:1-5)

Seeking God's salvation is the work of the Holy Spirit. We have the assurance that it is effective in 1 Corinthians 15.

> 'There is a natural body, and there is a spiritual body. And so it is written, "The first man Adam became a living being." The last Adam became a life-giving spirit. However, the spiritual is not first, but the natural, and afterwards the spiritual. The first man was of the earth, made of dust; the second Man is the Lord from heaven. As was the man of dust, so also are those who are made of dust; and as is the heavenly Man, so also are those who are heavenly. And as we have borne the image of the man of dust, we shall also bear the image of the heavenly Man.' (1 Corinthians 15:44-49)

Scripture says the sacrifice is applicable to any – any individual who repents and turns to God (Ephesians 2); to include all of human life:

> 'Therefore remember, that you, once Gentiles in the flesh – who are called Uncircumcision by what is called the Circumcision made in the flesh by hands – that at that time you were without Christ, being aliens from the commonwealth of Israel and strangers from the covenants of promise, having no hope and without God in the world. But now in Christ Jesus you who once were far off have been brought near by the blood of Christ.' (Ephesians 2:11-13)

God the Son's obedience to God the Father, to death on a cross – the shedding of holy blood, and the Resurrection through God the Holy Spirit was the healing Work of the Blessed Trinity.

> 'Who, in the days of His flesh, when He had offered up prayers and supplications, with vehement cries and tears to Him who was able to save Him from death, and was heard because of His godly fear, though He was a Son, yet He learned obedience by the things which He suffered. And having been perfected, He became the author of eternal salvation to all who obey Him.' (Hebrews 5:7-9)

Chapter 17 - The Blood and the Holy Spirit

The New Testament was written by various apostles. These apostles would not have known the astounding truths, for instance about Jesus' death on the cross being a total and wonderful sacrifice for human sin, the sin of the whole world, unless the Holy Spirit had taught them this wonderful truth. It was a wonderful truth because all their experience was with the person of Jesus during His earthly life, and His death and resurrection, and these truths about Him mean both God and Man in total harmony within Himself would not have been known to them from a normal human point of view.

We see that the Holy Spirit takes the actual life of Jesus on earth and makes it a real experience for the apostles in a wonderful way even after He has ascended into Heaven. The Holy Spirit glorifies the ascended Christ; we know that for certain by the power of the Holy Spirit, that He has ascended on high to the right hand of God and everything – His angels, archangels, things past, things present, things to come are subject unto Him. This wonderful truth could not have been known to the apostles, or us, by our finite minds but is enjoined by Jesus - the Holy Spirit makes this wonderful truth about Jesus real to us, that He is reigning supreme, despite the world being in chaos and ruins, in many ways in a mess as we can see every day.

The Holy Spirit also takes the death of Jesus and makes known to us the truth of the fact that Jesus' death was a wonderful sacrifice for the sins of the whole world. He makes it so real to us that we say that the blood of Jesus washes white as snow, making our sins, which are as scarlet, as white as wool, as we read in Isaiah 1:18, in prophecy of what Jesus' death would mean:

> 'Though your sins are like scarlet, they shall be as white as snow; though they are red like crimson, they shall be as wool.'

The Holy Spirit also makes known to us the fact of the risen Christ as a reality in our lives, so that we can say,

> 'He lives, He lives, Christ Jesus lives today. He walks with me and talks with me along life's narrow way. He lives, He lives, salvation to impart. You ask me how I know He lives: He lives within my heart.'
> (Alfred Henry Ackley, 1887-1960)

The Holy Spirit even takes the healing ministry of Jesus and makes it real as we pray and say the prayer of faith. It is Jesus, not man, but Jesus in the power of the Holy Spirit, and by the power of His blood, that makes a person whole in body, mind, and spirit, taking the name of Jesus as powerful in itself to achieve its end. So, the Holy Spirit takes the things that pertain to Jesus and His life and ministry and makes them very real to us in the twenty-first century as we live in a scientific and technological age. As we walk with God, we discover this truth to be real in our experience in our finite lives.

The Holy Spirit, we find in our experience, and in the teaching of the epistles, helps us in our infirmities, especially in our prayers, and He takes our prayers, the things that we utter, and takes them with groaning which cannot be uttered, into the presence of the Father; so He aids our prayers.

The Holy Spirit also guides us in our daily lives and our walk with the Lord. In the Acts of the Apostles, Paul was thinking about going to mission in another country, part of the Roman Empire, but was forbidden by the Holy Spirit, as we read in Acts 16:6,

> 'Now when they had gone through Phrygia and the region of Galatia, they were forbidden by the Holy spirit to preach the word in Asia.'

It is a truth that we experience in our daily lives. Certainly, in my ministry I have found that I do not always know why I am in a particular place at a particular time, but the Holy Spirit in fact shows me why I am there. For example, on one occasion I was told by the NHS (National Health Service in the UK) that I would have to go for treatment to help my wounded knee to get better in a hospital in Spalding in Lincolnshire. I reiterated to the various health professionals several times that I did not want to go to this particular hospital because it was far away from my friends, and I would have had very few visitors; being in Spalding Community Hospital, I knew I would feel lonely. Nevertheless, I undertook to go and on the second day, as I was sitting on a chair beside my bed, a man with a badge on his chest came and sat near me. He said he was the assistant chaplain of the hospital and he had wanted to meet me for a long time because I had helped him in his spiritual life, by laying on of hands given to him in the Lord - a powerful ministry to His people. In the end, six men like this came to see me as I was in that hospital and I realised I was there by the wonderful guidance of God through the work of the Holy Spirit, despite my misgivings.

We may also find, as we realise that God is within us, that we even meet people who we haven't intended to, or haven't known would ever meet, not even known of their existence or their name, but we may find ourselves with them in a particular way and realise that God has planned that we should meet at a particular time and for a particular purpose which is revealed to us later. This is exactly what happened to Philip in the Acts of the Apostles:

> 'Now an angel of the Lord spoke to Philip, saying, "Arise and go toward the south along the road which goes down from Jerusalem to Gaza." This is desert. So he arose and went. And behold, a man of Ethiopia, a eunuch of great authority under Candace the queen of the Ethiopians, who had charge of all her treasury, and had come to Jerusalem to worship, was returning. And sitting in his chariot, he was reading Isaiah the prophet. Then the Spirit said to Philip, "Go near and overtake this chariot." So Philip ran to him, and heard him reading the prophet Isaiah, and said, "Do you understand what you are reading?" And he said, "How can I, unless someone guides me?" And he asked Philip to come up and sit with him. The place in the Scripture which he read was this: "He was led as a sheep to the slaughter; and as a lamb before its hearer is silent, so He opened not His mouth. In His humiliation His justice was taken away, and who will declare His generation? For His life is taken from the earth." So the eunuch answered Philip and said, "I ask you, of whom does the prophet say this, of himself or of some other man?" Then Philip opened his mouth,

and beginning at this Scripture, preached Jesus to him.' (Acts 8:26-35)

On another occasion, I was on a weekend holiday staying in a hotel. On one morning, we heard a lady singing to the accompaniment of a piano and we decided we would like to stay there and listen. However, because it was such a very good programme, there were no seats available for us to sit on. A lady, seeing our needs, said,
"You can have my seat, but I will be very slow in getting up because I have such a terrible pain in my back; I have had it for many years because an operation on my back injured it and went wrong." I took hold of her hand and said to her, I'm sure guided by the Spirit,
"Do you realise your back could be completely healed and that you will be free of pain by breakfast tomorrow morning?" She said,
"How can that be?" I said,
"Just believe it will happen," as I took hold of her hand and prayed a simple prayer quietly. She got up and we went in and sat down. The next morning, she was at the door of the breakfast room to meet us, and she said,
"My back is completely free of pain, after so many months of terrible agony; it's so wonderful, even the injury has been healed." I said,
"We praise the Lord Jesus for this healing." Then she said,
"What about my husband?" so I said,
"What about him?" She said,
"He can't walk; he can't stand, and he would like you to pray with him. He's over there lying on the sofa." So, I went to this man and said,
"Do you want me to pray for you?" And he said,

"Please." So I prayed a prayer of faith quietly with him. He stood up and found he could walk for the first time for some years. The next morning, we were getting into a taxi to journey home and there were the two of them, man and wife, standing near the taxi and they said how wonderful it was that they had met us on their holiday. I call these 'Godincidences'; meetings with others planned for a particular purpose and guided by the Holy spirit Himself.

So every day I pray, "Lord, this day may I this be doing the right thing in the right place for the right reason." This prayer of mine is so often and so wonderfully answered, yet still I am taken by surprise when it is wonderfully put into effect by the Holy Spirit. Praise the Lord!

PART FOUR

The Conclusion

Chapter 18 – Partaking of the finished Work of God

My own life has been a testimony to the experience of God's healing power, even from childhood up to the present day in my ninetieth year. I do not say that I have never been sick, in fact in all my life I have frequently been sick or ill, and am now infirm, but nevertheless, God has continually healed me throughout my life. My experience of Divine Healing, through my ministry as a church minister, dates back to the time when I was given an angelic commission to do this on May 10th, 1969.

I can testify that healing miracles began to be seen at St Paul's Church, Hainault, Essex, England, in the Diocese of Chelmsford. Accounts of these can be found in my book 'The God of Miracles'. Healing can, however, can also be gradual; just as medical treatment and healing is gradual, Divine Healing, though still miraculous, can be gradual, taking time to take apparent effect from the time of ministry.

It is important to note that healing from God is not limited to conditions of individual illness such as terminal conditions but spans a wide spectrum of healing. Divine healing includes healing of emotions, healing of broken relationships such as marriages, healing from demonic powers or possession (in Greek being demonised), and of paramount importance, healing of the spirit to salvation. In Matthew's Gospel, in the Sermon on the Mount, Jesus emphasised the importance of healing relationships with others, including in marriage, as we read in Chapter 5 verses 21-22 and 27-28:

"You have head that it was said to those of old, 'You shall not murder, and whoever murders will be in danger of the judgement.' But I say to you that whoever is angry with his brother without cause shall be in danger of the judgement." And "You have heard that it was said to those of old, 'You shall not commit adultery.' But I say to you that whoever looks at a woman to lust for her has already committed adultery with her in his heart."

Paul, when he was writing to the Ephesians, also taught about the healing of relationships within the body of the church, quoting from Zechariah 8:16 and Psalm 4:4, as we see in chapter 4 verses 25-27:

> 'Therefore, putting away lying, 'let each one of you speak truth with his neighbour,' for we are members of one another. 'Be angry and do not sin', do not let the sun go down on your wrath, nor give place to the devil.'

All of God's activities and purposes can be seen as a healing work that will lead ultimately to the healing of nations, to salvation and everlasting life, as we read in Isaiah, Ezekiel, John's Gospel, and Revelation:

> 'Therefore, with joy you will draw water from the wells of salvation.' (Isaiah 12:3)

> 'Then the eyes of the blind shall be opened, and the ears of the deaf shall be unstopped. Then the lame shall leap like a deer, and the tongue of the dumb

sing. For waters shall burst forth in the wilderness, and streams in the desert.' (Isaiah 35:5-6)

'Then he said to me: 'This water flows toward the eastern region, goes down into the valley, and enters the sea. When it reaches the sea, its waters are healed. And it shall be that every living thing that moves, wherever the rivers go, will live. There will be a very great multitude of fish, because these waters go there; for they will be healed, and everything will live wherever the river goes.' (Ezekiel 47:8-9)

"But whoever drinks of the water that I shall give him will never thirst. But the water that I shall give him will become in him a fountain of water springing up into everlasting life." (John 4:14)

'And he showed me a pure river of water of life, clear as crystal, proceeding from the throne of God and of the Lamb. In the middle of its street, and on either side of the river, was the tree of life, which bore twelve fruits, each tree yielding its fruit every month. The leaves of the tree were for the healing of the nations.' (Revelation 22:1-2)

In the New Testament, the Greek word 'sozo', used when Jesus has healed someone, physically, emotionally, or spiritually, translated as 'save', can also mean deliver, make whole, restore and heal. Paul used the word 'sozo' when he was writing to the Corinthians:

> 'For since, in the wisdom of God, the world through wisdom did not know God, it pleased God through the foolishness of the message preached to save those who believe.' (1 Corinthians 1:21)

We can see that God's purpose in an individual is not simply to heal a physical condition or sickness, but to bring every person who responds to His act of Salvation into 'wholeness'. That is, the complete healing or sanctification of the whole person, body, mind, and spirit.

> 'Now may the God of peace Himself sanctify you completely; and may your whole spirit, soul, and body be preserved blameless at the coming of our Lord Jesus Christ.' (1 Thessalonians 5:23)

I think if we could say that God has priorities, it would be first the healing of the spirit, second the healing of the mind, and thirdly the healing of the body, in that order. Or, remembering that man is made in His image, as a kind of pale reflection of the trinity, perhaps we cannot prioritise or separate any of these three elements that represent the essence of humanity. God's healing purpose of wholeness is seen as the fulfilment of His Kingdom, after Christ's return and after the judgement, in Christians possessing a new spiritual body that is without any sickness, pain, sorrow or weeping, and there is to be no more death in the fulfilled Kingdom.

> "And God will wipe away every tear from their eyes; there shall be no more pain, for the former things have passed away." (Revelation 21:4)

God's purpose in healing is seen supremely in the ministry of His Son, our Lord Jesus Christ, who is said, in all His actions and ministry, to be fulfilling God's purpose. In the New Testament He is called the 'image of the invisible God', and it also states that in Him dwells all the fullness of the Godhead in bodily form:

> 'He is the image of the invisible God, the firstborn over all creation.' (Colossians 1:15)

> 'For it pleased the Father that in Him all the fulness should dwell.' (Colossians 1:19)

In the Gospels, we see Jesus as being in command of natural forces, such as stilling the storm on the Sea of Galilee, and His command even of food, a material thing, in feeding five thousand people with loaves and fish (see John 6:1-14). We also see His complete victory over death in the city of Nain, raising a widow's son on the way to his funeral, absolutely dead, raised back to life (see Luke 7:11-17), and of course the familiar account of the raising of His friend Lazarus, brother of Mary and Martha, from the dead (see John 11:38-44). The epistles of the New Testament also focus on the power if God in every way, and especially healing.

> 'How good is the God we adore!
> Our faithful, unchangeable friend:
> His love is as great as his power
> And knows neither measure nor end.
>
> For Christ is the first and the last;
> His Spirit will guide us safe home;

> We'll praise Him for all that is past
> And trust Him for all that's to come.'
> Joseph Hart (1712-1768)

The fulfilment of God's purpose for the world is seen in the cessation of war and fighting, at which time nations will no longer rise against each other. Se we can see the work of the United Nations, in all its aspects, including feeding the poor, providing vaccines against deadly diseases and plagues, as the work of God and should be prayed for. So all medical work, especially in the poorer nations, is seen to be flowing with the healing work of God.

> 'He shall judge between the nations, and rebuke many people; they shall beat their swords into ploughshares, and their spears into pruning hooks; nation shall not lift up sword against nation, neither shall they learn war anymore.' (Isaiah 2:4)

> 'Rejoice greatly, O daughter of Zion! Shout, O daughter of Jerusalem! Behold, your King is coming to you; He is just and having salvation, lowly and riding on a donkey, a colt, the foal of a donkey. I will cut off the chariot from Ephraim and the horse from Jerusalem; the battle bow shall be cut off. He shall speak peace to the nations; His dominion shall be from sea to sea, and from the River to the ends of the earth.' (Zechariah 9:9-10)

So we have seen that the only way that the human race, and even the whole of creation, could be healed was by the great sacrifice of Jesus Christ. We have seen that its effect applies to all the ages since the beginning of creation by the work of the Holy Spirit, applying it to sick conditions in human beings and the creation at large. The process of healing effected by Yahweh Rapha is a gradual one for the whole of His creation. I want to stress, however, that for the Holy Spirit to become effective for God's healing, certain conditions have to be met:

> 1. Believe in God and believe in His pure love
> 2. Ask God for healing and believe it is taking place (faith) in actions that further God's holy purposes. This can be through the Holy Spirit or through health professionals.

I have found, in my life's experience, that churches, when they say prayers for the sick, seem to think that they have to somehow persuade God to heal the people on their prayer list. But God does not need persuading to heal, for He has declared Himself a healer:

> "If you diligently heed the voice of the Lord your God and do what is right in His sight, give ear to His commandments and keep all His statutes, I will put none of the diseases on you which I have brought on the Egyptians. **For I am the Lord who heals you**." (Exodus 15:26)

It is important to understand that total healing is Yahweh Rapha's eternal and enduring work. God's remedy for Adam's sin and its consequences was effected through what theologians term the passion and sacrifice of His only son. Jesus Himself envisaged this in the words He spoke at the Last Supper, as quoted earlier:

> "This is My blood of the new covenant, which is shed for many for the remission of sins." (Matthew 26:28)

This sacrifice restored the filial relationship between God and man, and in so doing enabled the foundational relationship of a new filial relationship once more between man and God. We can see the reality of the relationship renewed between God and man in which God Himself took the initiative, spelt out many times in the epistles by the apostles, written in such words as:

> 'For to this you were called, because Christ also suffered for us, leaving us an example, that you should follow in His steps: "Who committed no sin, nor was deceit found in His mouth"; who, when He was reviled, did not revile in return; when He suffered, He did not threaten, but committed Himself to Him who judges righteously; who Himself bore our sins in His own body on the tree, that we, having died to sins, might live for righteousness – by whose stripes we are healed.' (1 Peter 2:21-24)

Paul describes Christ's healing work on the cross, that resulted in the abrogation, or we might say the repeal, of the sentence of spiritual death in his first epistle to the Church at Corinth. He makes it absolutely clear that this work was not achieved only through the blood of the sacrifice, but also through the glorious resurrection, without which, he says, our faith is futile; the conquering of death itself was effected through the resurrection of Christ.

> 'Now if Christ is preached that He has been raised from the dead, how do some among you say that there is no resurrection of the dead? But if there is no resurrection of the dead, then Christ is not risen. And if Christ is not risen, then our preaching is empty and your faith is also empty. Yes, and we are found false witnesses of God, because we have testified of God that He raised up Christ, whom He did not raise up – if in fact the dead do not rise. For if the dead do not rise, then Christ is not risen. And if Christ is not risen, your faith is futile; you are still in your sins!' (1 Corinthians 15:12-17)

So not only was sin forgiven and its guilt taken forever away, but the barrier between God and man was now gone, and that was, and indeed is, the greatest and deepest healing possible. This barrier between God and man was represented in the Temple from the time of the Exodus in the form of a curtain or veil that separated the holiest of holies.

> "You shall make a veil woven of blue, purple, and scarlet thread, and fine woven linen. It shall be woven with an artistic design of cherubim. You shall hang it upon the four pillars of acacia wood overlaid with gold. Their hooks shall be gold, upon four sockets of silver. And you shall hang the veil from the clasps. Then you shall bring the ark of the Testimony in there, behind the veil. The veil shall be a divider for you between the holy place and the Most holy.' (Exodus 26:31-33)

We can see from Mark's Gospel that at the moment of Christ's death that this barrier between God and man, this veil that separated us, was gone; it was torn in two:

> 'And Jesus cried out with a loud voice and breathed His last. Then the veil of the temple was torn in two from top to bottom.' (Mark 15:37-38)

The writer to the Hebrews spells out this teaching in chapter 9. The way to into the Holiest of All was only symbolic in the first tabernacle, when the high priest went through the veil once a year with sacrificial blood which he offered for himself and for the people for their sins committed in ignorance. But Christ came as High Priest with the perfect sacrifice:

> 'Not with the blood of goats and calves, but with His own blood He entered the Most Holy Place once for all, having obtained eternal redemption.' (Hebrews 9:12)

So God demonstrated His love towards us in that while we were yet sinners Christ died for us. This is the eternal healing work of Yahweh Rapha.

When we think of a human physician, we would apply that term to someone who will treat a patient who needs healing of the body. Genesis records that when God created Adam, He created a perfect man in regards to his health; Adam had no sickness, decay, pain, or death. But because of sin, even today, man's sicknesses are due to the fallen body. In the Genesis account, this was seen first as the pain of childbirth, then the struggle against creation:

> "I will greatly multiply your sorrow and your conception; in pain you shall bring forth children." (Genesis 3:16)
>
> "Cursed is the ground for your sake; in toil you shall eat of it all the days of your life." (Genesis 3:17)

It is important to say that, and we must acknowledge that, the wonders of medical science, the care of doctors and nurses and other health professionals etc are God given. Nevertheless, there are times when God will still heal the physical body after prayer through faith. This, in my experience, is often with the laying on of hands as Jesus was requested to do in Mark's Gospel:

> 'And behold, one of the rulers of the synagogue came, Jairus by name. And when he saw Him, he fell at His feet and begged Him earnestly, saying, "My little daughter lies at the point of death. Come and lay your hands on her, that she may be healed, and she will live." (Mark 5:22-23)

James, in his epistle to the church, gave instructions for how to prayer for those who are sick. This included praying over them and anointing them with oil in the name of Jesus:

> 'Is anyone among you sick? Let him call for the elders of the church, and let them pray over him, anointing him with oil in the name of the Lord. And the prayer of faith will save the sick, and the Lord

will raise him up. And if he has committed sins, he will be forgiven.' (James 5:14-15)

We do have to accept that not all people are healed, and only God knows why. Paul himself suffered from what he called, in his letter to the Corinthians, his 'thorn in the flesh', declaring that he would rather keep the infirmity if by it God's grace in him is greater.

> 'And lest I should be exalted above measure by the abundance of the revelations, a thorn in the flesh was given to me, a messenger of Satan to buffet me, lest I be exalted above measure. Concerning this thing I pleaded with the Lord three times that it might depart from me. And He said to me, "My grace is sufficient for you, for My strength is made perfect in weakness." Therefore most gladly I will rather boast in my infirmities, that the power of Christ may rest upon me. Therefore, I take pleasure in infirmities, in reproaches, in needs, in persecutions, in distresses, for Christ's sake. For when I am weak, then I am strong.' (2 Corinthians 12:7)

We also have physicians and health professionals who are trained to treat those who need healing of the mind; those with mental-health issues. Symptoms for these conditions are rarely simply physical. Jesus Himself healed more than just the physical diseases or sickness of the people during His earthly ministry, including, according to Matthew's Gospel, those who were afflicted with torments:

> 'And Jesus went about all Galilee, teaching in their synagogues, preaching the gospel of the kingdom, and healing all kinds of sickness and all kinds of disease among the people. Then His fame went throughout all Syria; and they brought to Him all sick people who were afflicted with various diseases and torments, and those who were demon-possessed, epileptics, and paralytics; and He healed them.' (Matthew 4:23-24)

In His ministry, Jesus demonstrated that God's will is to heal all who come to Him in faith. God's will for us all is that we should be well in body, mind, and spirit. His healing goes down even to the subconscious mind. For a more detailed discussion of divine healing for the mind, see my book 'God and Healing of the Mind'. Towards the close of His earthly ministry Jesus bequeathed His peace to mankind with the words:

> "Peace I leave with you, My peace I give to you; not as the world gives do I give to you. Let not your heart be troubled, neither let it be afraid.' (John 14:27)

Yahweh Rapha's cosmic act of rescue, His healing work through the incarnation of Jesus and the work of the Holy spirit demonstrates His enduring and eternal love for fallen humanity and creation.

Summary

In summary, I would like to remind the reader of the testimony of my own life's experience in ministry of the healing work of God that I can testify to as being true. I know, and many hundreds have witnessed, that thousands have been healed in many ways: the deaf hearing, the lame walking, immoveable limbs freed, crutches abandoned, addictions and phobias eradicated, countless set free, converted to Christ and empowered for effective spiritual living.

So, we know that for God's cosmic healing work to become possible there are four essential foundations needed: correct belief, belief in God, belief in God as Creator, and understanding the creation of human beings. This last foundation is understanding the fall of Adam and Eve and the terrible consequences of disease, illness, infirmity, and death, and the fall of the natural order which became alien to mankind and against which mankind has to struggle.

Having understood the beginning and the consequences, it is essential to grasp and understand God's great act of rescue, confirmed in heaven, and born of the Father's love for His creation. We must understand, acknowledge, and give thanks for the incarnation, believing that Jesus paid the price. He steadfastly went to the cross and paid the ultimate sacrifice which was needed to rescue mankind from sickness, and to restore the world – nature, to its original plan. There could be no healing for anything in creation apart from this act which overcame sin and death and made the restoration of the natural order possible.

The effect of this great sacrifice to heal man and restore the whole of creation is the working of the Holy Spirit (washed in the blood). So, the great rescue act is confirmed by the loving heart of God, made operative by the death of Jesus, God's Son. Finally, it is essential that prayer for healing is made in faith. It is faith that opens the door for Yahweh Rapha to heal.

> "Have faith in God. For assuredly, I say to you, whoever says to this mountain, 'Be removed and be cast into the sea,' and does not doubt in his heart, but believes that those things he says will be done, he will have whatever he says. Therefore I say to you, whatever things you ask when you pray, believe that you receive them, and you will have them." (Mark 11:22-24)

So now we see that human beings can be made perfectly whole and never die. And the natural order is now subject to His will. So, the healing of the planet can only be effected by the work of God as it is applied to the endemic disease of sin through the fulfilment of Yahweh Rapha's great work; His healing work described as making all things new.

> 'Then He who sat on the throne said, "Behold, I make all things new." And He said to me, "Write, for these words are true and faithful." And He said to me, "It is done! I am the Alpha and the Omega, the Beginning and the End. I will give of the fountain of the water of life freely to him who thirsts. He who overcomes shall inherit all things, and I will be his God and he shall be My son." (Revelation 21:5-7)

Appendix 1

The Nicene Creed

We believe in one God,
The Father, the Almighty,
Maker of heaven and earth
Of all that is, seen and unseen.

We believe in one Lord, Jesus Christ,
The only Son of God,
Eternally begotten of the Father,
God from God, Light from Light,
True God from true God,
Begotten, not made,
Of one Being with the Father.
Through Him all things were made.

For us and our salvation
He came down from heaven:
By the power of the Holy Spirit
He became incarnate from the Virgin Mary,
And was made man.

For our sake He was crucified under Pontius Pilate;
He suffered death and was buried.
On the third day he rose again
In accordance with the Scriptures;
He ascended into heaven
And is seated at the right hand of the Father.

He will come again in glory to judge the living and the dead,
And His kingdom will have no end.

We believe in the Holy Spirit, the Lord, the giver of life,
Who proceeds from the Father and the Son.
With the Father and the Son He is worshipped and glorified.
He has spoken through the Prophets.
We believe in one holy catholic and apostolic Church.
We acknowledge one baptism for the forgiveness of sins.
We look for the resurrection of the dead,
And the life of the world to come.

Amen.

    Adopted at the First Council of Nicaea 19th June 325AD.

www.ingramcontent.com/pod-product-compliance
Lightning Source LLC
LaVergne TN
LVHW030636080426
835510LV00023B/3388